Contemporary's
Essentials of Reading

Book 5

Contemporary's
Essentials of Reading
Book 5

McGraw Hill **Wright Group**

Photo and Art Credits

Computer art created by Jim Blanton; Cover Peter Griffith/Masterfile; 5 Michael Collier;
11 courtesty Wendy's International; 13 courtesy KFC; 19 Tim Courlas;
22 Doug Martin; 30 Aaron Haupt; 41 David R. Frazier Photolibrary;
50, 58 Aaron Haupt; 68 SuperStock; 79, 85 Aaron Haupt; 96 Joseph A. DiChello;
106 from Fables, Arnold Lobel, HarperCollins Publishers 1980.
Used by permission. All rights reserved.

Permission Acknowledgment

Unabridged text and illustrations titled: "The Poor Old Dog."
Copyright © 1980 by Arnold Lobel. Used by permission of HarperCollins Publishers.

ISBN: 0-07-282264-3

Send all inquiries to:
Wright Group/McGraw-Hill
130 E. Randolph, Suite 400
Chicago, IL 60601

Printed in the United States of America.

5 6 7 8 9 10 QPD 08

The **McGraw·Hill** Companies

The editorial staff wishes to gratefully acknowledge the contributions of the following advisors, reviewers, and writers, whose considerable efforts, suggestions, ideas, and insights helped to make this text a more valuable and viable learning tool.

Advisory Board for the *McGraw-Hill/Contemporary Essentials of Reading Series*

JoAnn Bukovich-Henderson
Director, Adult Education
SE Regional Resource Center
Juneau, Alaska

Dr. William Walker
Assistant Superintendent
Adult Basic Education
Knox County Schools
Knoxville, Tennessee

Nancy Wilson-Webb
Co-op Director
Adult Basic Education
Fort Worth ISD Consortium
Fort Worth, Texas

Contributing Writers

Elizabeth Shupe
ABE/ESL Instructor
Right to Read of Weld County
Greeley, Colorado

Dr. Nancy Burkhalter
Language and Literacy Consultant
Laramie, Wyoming

Dr. Nora Ruth Roberts
Composition and Literature Instructor
Hunter College—Medgar Evers
   Affiliate of CUNY
New York, New York

Gail Rice
Palos Heights, Illinois

Laura Belgrave
Largo, Florida

Doug Hutzelman
Kettering, Ohio

Christina Hutzelman
Kettering, Ohio

Mary Frances Harper
Director of the Literacy Council
   of Grant County
Sheridan, Arkansas

Clarita D. Henderson
Educational Consultant
Buffalo, New York

Susan Paull McShane
Executive Director
Literacy Volunteer of America
   Charlottesville-Albemarle
Charlottesville, Virginia

Patricia Costello
ABE/ESL Instructor
San Francisco City College
San Francisco, California

Carole Gerber
Columbus, Ohio

Reviewers

Connie J. Dodd
ABE Instructor
Frontier Central School District
Hamburg, New York

Julie Gerson
Coordinator
Goodwill Literacy Institute
Pittsburgh, Pennsylvania

Dr. Patricia Kuhel
English/Reading Facilitator
Labette Community College
Parsons, Kansas

Rubianna M. Porter
Director of Precollege Programs
Cleveland State Community College
Cleveland, Tennessee

Laura Weidner, Director
Applied Technology and Apprenticeship
Catonsville Community College
Catonsville, Maryland

Table of Contents

Nutrition, Health, and Safety

Workplace Skills

The Reading Corner

NAME _____ Pretest for Book 5

A. Put a √ next to the synonyms for the first word.

1. happy   a. ____ unhappy   b. ____ glad   c. ____ joyful

2. near   a. ____ far   b. ____ close   c. ____ distant

B. Put a √ next to the antonyms for the first word.

3. noise   a. ____ loud   b. ____ quiet   c. ____ peaceful

4. cheerful   a. ____ sad   b. ____ happy   c. ____ gloomy

C. Put a √ next to the best answer.

5. Carla works in the post office. She sells _____ to mail the letters.

   a. ____ packages   b. ____ tickets   c. ____ stamps

6. Greg parked the _____ in the garage.

   a. ____ ladder   b. ____ barrel   c. ____ truck

7. The baby was cold and wanted her _____.

   a. ____ toy   b. ____ blanket   c. ____ rattle

D. Write the letter C on the line if the word is a compound word. Put a √ on the line if the word is not a compound word.

8. storytime ____   9. worthwhile ____   10. afternoon ____

11. graceful ____   12. wishbone ____   13. quickly ____

E. Put a √ next to the word that fits the meaning of the sentence.

14. Jay _____ his bike to school.

   a. ____ road   b. ____ rode

15. You could _____ the storm clouds in the sky.

   a. ____ sea   b. ____ see

16. The _____ on the car gave out.

   a. ____ brake   b. ____ break

1

F. Read the story. Put a √ next to the best answer.

Frontier Days started on September 23, 1897. A cannon was fired. Bells rang. Train whistles blew. Many local people fired their guns, too. This was the start of the biggest rodeo event ever. It was born in Cheyenne, Wyoming.

People came from all over the country to attend. Special train sleeping cars were used as hotels. The Union Pacific Railroad offered special rates. Round-trip tickets to Cheyenne from Denver, Colorado, cost $2.

People entered the fairgrounds free of charge. It cost them 15 cents to sit in an uncovered bleacher for the rodeo events. A grandstand seat cost them 35 cents. The first Frontier Days had 11 rodeo events. The rodeo was always the most popular part of Frontier Days. Those 11 contests are still held today.

17. What was the story mostly about?

    a. _____ People traveling on the train from Denver to Cheyenne

    b. _____ The start of the biggest rodeo

    c. _____ The cost to attend Frontier Days

18. What does the sentence "It was born in Cheyenne, Wyoming," mean in the first paragraph?

    a. _____ Frontier Days began there.

    b. _____ Wyoming became a state.

    c. _____ Union Pacific Railroad began there.

19. What was the cost of a grandstand seat?

    a. _____ 15 cents

    b. _____ $2

    c. _____ 35 cents

20. Frontier Days

    a. _____ ended in 1897.

    b. _____ is still held today.

    c. _____ has 10 rodeo events.

A Visit to the Library

Have you ever gone to a library? Do you have a library card? Read about Justo's visit to the library.

Justo's Big Problem

Justo Perez stomped into the house and slammed the door behind him. He threw his book bag on the table and looked at his mother. "I hate school, and I hate the fifth grade!"

"Justo, that's no way to talk," said his mother. Rita Perez had been home from work for ten minutes. Her day had been difficult, and she was tired. She had just changed out of her waitress uniform. She said to her son, "Now tell me what happened to make you so angry."

The boy's shoulders **slumped.** "I'm sorry, Mama," he said. "I have to write a report about birds that live in the rain forest. It's due Monday. Fred gets to write about rain forest snakes. Sue Lee gets to write about rain forest cats. But I'm stuck with birds. I don't know anything about them. It's not fair!" said Justo.

slumped *moved downwards*

Justo **admitted** that his teacher had given him the homework a week ago. "I was just too busy," Justo said. "Now it's Friday and the school library is closed. I'll never get enough information. We don't even own an **encyclopedia.**"

admitted *told*

For a minute, Mrs. Perez didn't say anything. She couldn't afford to buy one book, never mind a whole encyclopedia. Her husband, Felipe, had been gone for three months. She was on her own now.

Mrs. Perez said none of that to Justo. She smiled at him, trying not to show the worry she felt. "Maybe it's time we visited the public library," she said. "I'll bet they have an encyclopedia there."

Scary From the Outside

Mrs. Perez had passed the library many times but had never gone inside. She had not finished school and didn't think she was a good reader. She was sure everyone would be able to tell. Now, as she and Justo stood before the building, she felt her heart begin to beat faster. Even her hands felt damp.

The library was very tall and made of old brick. Vines curled around the sides. Mrs. Perez hoped she was dressed all right for a building that looked so important. She took a deep breath. At last, she opened the door.

Friendly on the Inside

"Can I help you?" said a voice behind them.

Mrs. Perez and Justo turned around. A woman with kind eyes smiled at them.

"I'm Aretha Jones," the woman said. "I'm a library **volunteer**. I'd be happy to help you find your way around."

Mrs. Perez **relaxed** a little and smiled back. She explained what Justo needed. "Would it be OK for us to look at an encyclopedia?" she asked.

"Sure," said Mrs. Jones. "An encyclopedia is a great place to start. But the library also has whole books about rain forest birds. We even have videotapes on the subject."

"Videos!" said Justo. He tugged on his mother's sleeve. "Wow, Mama! Isn't that great?"

Mrs. Perez blushed. "I'm sorry, Justo," she said. "I don't have money to rent a video."

"Oh, don't worry about that," said Mrs. Jones. "Borrowing books and videos is free. All you need is a library card. I'll get you an **application** form after I get you started here."

An Information Store

Mrs. Perez and Justo spent a half-hour with Mrs. Jones. They explored many rooms. Justo loved the children's section. He quickly picked out two books on rain forest birds. Then they picked out a video on the subject.

application *a form written out to give information about a person*

Mrs. Jones explained that library books were given special numbers, then put on shelves by those numbers. She showed Mrs. Perez and Justo how to use the numbers to find books on the shelves.

"Once you get the hang of it, you can use the numbers to find almost any book you want," Mrs. Jones said. "Oh! You also can listen to newspapers, telephone books, and cassettes. We even have computers you can use."

merchandise
*items for sale
through stores or
catalogs*

It struck Mrs. Perez that the library was like a huge store. But instead of selling **merchandise,** it gave information. She grinned to herself. This was a lot like shopping, only better. She didn't have to open her wallet just to try out something.

"Many people don't know that the library also has special events," said Mrs. Jones. "We have tutors to help adults improve their reading, programs on history and nature, and many fun things for children to do. Goodness, there is always something going on here. And it doesn't cost a dime."

faucet *water tap*

Later, Mrs. Perez used the number system to find a book about fixing faucets. The kitchen **faucet** dripped all the time. It needed repair fast! Then, just for fun, she picked out a book of short stories. She even found a book on finding a job. Mrs. Perez enjoyed her visit to the library so much she knew she wanted her own library card.

Mrs. Jones gave Mrs. Perez an application form to fill out for her card. The library card wasn't fancy, but it was hers. Holding it made her feel proud.

Not Just Homework

It was almost dark when Mrs. Perez and Justo got home with the video and the books they had checked out.

"I can't believe that place," Justo said. "The library has everything we'll ever need!"

"Not quite," said Mrs. Perez. She winked at Justo. "It doesn't have anyone to write your report. You still have to do that yourself."

Justo groaned. "I almost forgot that our library visit was because of my homework."

"As a matter of fact," Mrs. Perez said softly, "the trip turned out to be more than that." She patted her son's hair. "Come on. Let's watch that video together."

Words, Words, Words

A. **Antonyms** are words with the opposite or almost opposite meaning; for example, *start* and *stop*. **Synonyms** are words that mean the same or almost the same; for example, *start* and *begin*. Find words in the story that are the antonyms for the words below. Write the words on the line. The first one is done for you.

1. easy   **difficult** _____

2. wife _____

3. frowned _____

4. ashamed _____

Find words from the story that are synonyms for the words below. Write the words on the line.

5. told _____

6. fix _____

7. teachers _____

8. calm _____

B. A **compound word** is a new word made by putting two other words together. *Football* is a compound word made by joining *foot* and *ball* together. Put a √ next to the compound words below.

1. _____ system   2. _____ nature   3. _____ homework

4. _____ darkness   5. _____ keyhole   6. _____ sailboat

7. _____ hallway   8. _____ public   9. _____ darkroom

Word Story:

In this book you will meet words about computers. When you talk about computer hardware, you are talking about the metal and plastic parts that make up a computer.

C. Read the sentences below. Write the word in each sentence that has the long vowel sound.

1. Justo enjoyed creating art with (clay, metal).

   _____

2. Maria (asked, prayed) for forgiveness.

   _____

3. Mrs. Perez served breakfast on a (tray, platter).

   _____

D. Read the sentences below. Circle the words that begin with the **shr** sound, like the word *shred*.

1. Justo shrugged when his mother asked him if he had watered the shrubs.

2. She said he could not depend on rain showers to keep the plants from shriveling up.

3. The shrubs were already starting to shrink.

E. A **suffix** is a group of letters added to the end of a word to change the meaning of the word. For example, the suffix **-ance** sometimes means action.
The word *assistance* means the *state of being assisted*. Add the suffix **-ance** to each word below and then write a sentence using each new word.

1. appear _____**appearance**_____

   _____**She has a nice appearance.**_____

2. perform _____

   _____

3. attend _____

   _____

Understanding

A. Read the questions below. Write your answers on the lines.

1. The story says that Mrs. Perez's husband, Felipe, has been gone for three months. How did her life change as a result?

   _____

2. The story does not say why Felipe is gone. Write possible reasons he may be gone. _____

   _____

3. The story does not say why Justo waited until the last minute to begin his report. Write reasons why he didn't get started sooner.

   _____

   _____

B. Read the questions below. Write your answers on the lines.

1. If Mrs. Perez had finished school, how might her life be different? _____

   _____

2. How might Mrs. Perez feel about visiting the library the next time she goes? _____

   _____

3. How might Mrs. Perez use the library to help her get a different job? _____

   _____

Discussion

A. Read the questions below. Write your answers on the lines.

1. Give two reasons why Mrs. Perez had not visited a library before.

   _____

   _____

2. What books did Mrs. Perez pick out for herself?

   _____

3. What did Justo and his mother learn to help them find books on the shelves?

   _____

   _____

B. Use the story to help you give answers.

1. Read the section "Justo's Big Problem" again. What was his mood when he first got home from school? _____

2. What was his mood after he talked to his mother? _____

   _____

3. What was his mood after he returned from the library? _____

   _____

C. Justo and his mother spent a lot of time at the library. Write about what they did from the time they entered to the time they left. Write it in the order that things happened.

   _____

   _____

LESSON 2

Meet Dave

This story is about Dave Thomas of Wendy's fast food.

Meet Dave

Almost everyone who watches TV has seen an ad for Wendy's fast-food restaurants. Dave Thomas is the man who stars in every commercial. However, Dave is more than the **spokesperson** for Wendy's. He is the one who came up with the idea for Wendy's and started this **fast-food chain**.

Dave's Early Childhood Years

Dave Thomas was born on July 2, 1932, in Atlantic City, New Jersey. Right after he was born, Dave was put up for **adoption,**

and at six weeks of age he was adopted by Rex and Auleva Thomas. His adopted mother, Auleva, died when Dave was only five years old. After her death, Dave and his father moved a lot. Rex and Dave moved from state to state so Rex could find work.

spokesperson *someone who tells about a place, a thing, an event, a company, or a product*

fast-food chain *restaurants that serve fast food in many different cities and have the same name and menu items*

adoption *the legal process of making a child who was not born to you part of your family*

As a child, Dave lived in many places and ate at many restaurants. He really enjoyed eating out. At a young age, Dave decided that he wanted to own a restaurant when he grew up.

Dave Starts Working

Because they moved many times, Dave often felt lonely as a child. Each time they moved he was the new kid on the block. This led him to dive into work at a young age. Dave started to work when he was 12. He delivered groceries in Knoxville, Tennessee. Before he was 13, he was at his second job. This time he worked at Walgreen's. He was fired from this job because his boss found out that Dave was not 16 years old.

He was still only 12 years old when he took a job at the Regas Restaurant. He was a hard worker. Sometimes he worked up to 12 hours in a shift. The Regas brothers, who owned the restaurant, treated Dave like family.

Leaving School

When Dave was 15, he was working in a restaurant in Indiana. His family was getting ready to move again. Dave decided to stay behind. He rented a room to live in and started working full-time. He dropped out of high school. He thought he could learn more by working than by going to school.

Many years later, he was able to get his GED diploma. Today his diploma hangs proudly in his home. In interviews, you will hear him talk about the importance of staying in school.

Dave's Adult Years

enlisted *those who joined the service*

Sometime later, Dave joined the army. He was one of the youngest men to manage an **enlisted** men's club. After he completed his enlistment, he went to work at the Hobby House. This restaurant was where he met a waitress named Lorraine. In 1954, they were married.

In 1956, Dave and his boss, Phil Clauss, opened a new restaurant. It was called the Ranch House. At the Ranch House, Dave met Colonel Sanders.

Colonel Sanders was the man who started the Kentucky Fried Chicken restaurants. Phil bought some Kentucky Fried Chicken restaurants. He asked Dave to work for him at Kentucky Fried Chicken.

Four of the stores that Phil bought were not doing well. Dave worked hard at all four of these stores. Soon all four were doing better. Phil bought four more Kentucky Fried Chicken stores. They also did well. Phil made Dave a part owner. In 1968, Phil and Dave sold the restaurants for over 1 million dollars. By the age of 35, Dave was a **millionaire**.

Dave was then ready to open his own restaurant. On November 15, 1969, Dave opened the first Wendy's Old Fashioned Hamburgers. This first restaurant was in Columbus, Ohio. He named it after his eight-year-old daughter. Her real name was Melinda Lou, but her older brothers and sisters called her Wendy.

millionaire
somebody who has a million or more dollars

In the beginning, Dave did not have many items on his menu. The first restaurant had hamburgers, chili, french fries, soft drinks, and **Frosties**.

Other restaurant owners did not think that Dave would do very well. Dave surprised them all. In 1973, Dave decided to sell his ideas for the Wendy's restaurants. This way, other people could also open and run Wendy's restaurants.

Franchising

Dave was **franchising** so much that in the first 100 months of doing business more than 1,000 Wendy's restaurants were opened. Today, Wendy's restaurants are found all over the United States. They are also found in 34 other countries. The idea that started out as one restaurant in Ohio has grown into more than 4,800 restaurants around the world.

Dave Today

Today, Dave keeps very busy with the **charities** he supports. He has given a lot of time and money to many charities. Some of the ones he has given to are St. Jude Children's Research Hospital in Memphis, Tennessee; Children's Hospital in Columbus, Ohio; Children's Home Society of Florida, and the Ohio State University Cancer Research Institute in Columbus, Ohio.

However, the cause that means the most to Dave is adoption. In 1990, Dave was asked by the White House to be a national spokesperson for child adoption. Dave Thomas is not only a wealthy businessman, he is also a generous person who believes in giving to people in need.

Words, Words, Words

A. A **contraction** is a short way to write two words. The word *isn't* is a contraction. It takes the place of the words *is not*. The apostrophe (') is used with a contraction. It stands in for the missing letters. In *isn't,* the apostrophe stands for the letter *o* in *not.* On the lines below, write the contraction for each pair of words; then use the contraction in a sentence.

1. do not _____

2. did not _____

3. should not _____

4. would not _____

5. could not _____

Word Story:

The software for a computer is the program or programs that give the directions that make the computer run.

B. The words *child's coat* show that the child owns the coat. Add **'s** to a word to show that something is owned. Read the words below. Use the **'s.**

1. the restaurant that belongs to Dave _____

2. the food that the cat eats _____

3. the toy that was given to Alec _____

4. the ribbons that belong to the girl _____

5. the bed that John sleeps in _____

6. the car that Grandfather drives _____

7. the book that Patrick owns _____

C. **Compound words** are words made up of two separate words. For example, *doghouse* is made up of the word *dog* and the word *house*. Write the compound words on the lines below. Then, write a sentence for four of the compound words.

1. bird + house = _____

2. bird + bath = _____

3. book + mark = _____

4. book + case = _____

5. check + list = _____

6. check + book = _____

7. _____

_____

8. _____

_____

9. _____

_____

10. _____

_____

D. Sometimes, two consonants together stand for one sound like the letters **wr** and **sc.** Use **wr** or **sc** to make a word in each sentence.

1. Bill used the _____issors to cut the paper.

2. I gave the _____ong answer for the third question on the test.

3. _____ience is Al's best subject.

4. Jilly broke her _____ist when she fell.

5. Jilly also pulled a mu_____le.

6. Did you see the terrible car _____eck on the highway?

Understanding

A. A **fact** is something that you know is true. An **opinion** is what you feel or believe. For example: People use ketchup on their hamburgers. This is a fact. Ketchup is better than mustard on a hamburger. This is an opinion.

Write **F** for fact or **O** for opinion on the lines below.

1. _____ Dave Thomas liked hamburgers.

2. _____ Dave often felt lonely as a child.

3. _____ Dave was adopted.

4. _____ Dave delivered groceries when he lived in Knoxville.

5. _____ Dave was careful with his money.

6. _____ Dave was the best grocery delivery boy in Knoxville.

B. Read the sentences. Find the best endings for them. Put a √ next to your choice.

1. On rainy days, I wear

   a. _____ an umbrella.   b. _____ a raincoat.

2. When I get very hungry, I go to the refrigerator and

   a. _____ get something to eat.

   b. _____ check the refrigerator door.

3. The hallway light went out

   a. _____ and I could see better.   b. _____ and I changed it.

4. Today is my brother's birthday. I will

   a. _____ visit my sister.   b. _____ give him a gift.

5. Tomorrow I have a math test. Tonight I will study

   a. _____ addition problems.   b. _____ about airplanes.

Discussion

A. Throughout his life, Dave Thomas held different jobs. Using the story to help you, write in the circles below some of the jobs Dave held.

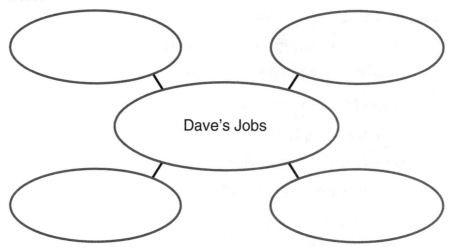

Dave's Jobs

B. You may have heard people talk about **cause** and **effect**. They are talking about the reason that makes or helps something else to happen. For example:

Cause: Because the first Wendy's restaurants were very successful,

Effect: Dave Thomas opened more.

Write on the lines below the effects for the causes given.

1. Cause: Because Dave's boss found out he was not 16 years old,

   Effect: _____

2. Cause: Because Dave worked hard at all four of the Kentucky Fried Chicken restaurants,

   Effect: _____

FAMILY LIFE

You Can Find the Information

In the story "A Visit to the Library" on page 3, Justo Perez had to do a report about birds that live in the rain forest. He and his mother went to the library. One of the places they found information was in an encyclopedia.

Look at the photo below. Do you know what statue is in the photo? It is the Statue of Liberty.

If you had to write a report about the Statue of Liberty, you might seek answers to such questions as:

- Where is this statue?
- Who designed it?
- When was it built?
- Why was it built?

Where would you look to find these answers?

You might try looking in an encyclopedia as Justo Perez did for his report. You might also find a book in the library written about this famous statue. Or if you use a computer, you might use the **Internet** for information. Now read some facts about the Statue of Liberty that appear below.

The Statue of Liberty was a gift to the United States from France. A man named Frédéric-Auguste Bartholdi designed it. He was born in France in August 1834.

The Statue of Liberty stands 151 feet and 1 inch from its base to its torch. Inside the statue, from its base to its torch, there are 171 steps. The statue weighs 225 tons.

The Statue of Liberty stands on a tiny island called Liberty Island. This island is in the New York Harbor. It has become a symbol of freedom for people who immigrate to the U.S.A. from other countries.

A. Write your answers on the line.

1. How much does the statue weigh?_____

2. Who designed it?_____

3. Where can you visit it?_____

B. Using an encyclopedia or another source of information, find out about the Golden Gate Bridge and the George Washington Bridge. Where are these bridges? When were they built?

_____

_____

_____

_____

LESSON 3

Learning More

Meet Sally and Jeff Hogan. They got married when they were very young.

Sally's Family

Sally's family was large. She had five brothers and two sisters. Her father and mother worked hard to **support** the family, but they still had money problems. There never seemed to be enough money to buy many of the things that other people had. When they needed food and clothing, they always shopped for sales and **bargains.** They could not spend much money for fun and games.

Sally's father and mother were always tired, and they did not have much time to talk with Sally or her brothers and sisters. They couldn't help her or the others with their schoolwork. They didn't understand the lessons.

support *help to pay bills*

bargains *items that are sold for less money*

Jeff's Family

Jeff and his family lived in the house next door to Sally's family. He had one brother and one sister. He wished he could help Sally, but his family had a hard time, too. His father had been **injured** in a car wreck when Jeff was nine years old. Now his father was not able to do much work. Jeff's mother kept a job to support the family while Jeff's father did what he could to help at home.

injured *hurt*

Jeff missed his mother because she worked long hours and was not at home most of the time. When she was at home, there was always a lot to do—cleaning the house, cooking, or washing the clothes. Jeff and his **siblings** helped when they could.

siblings *brothers and sisters*

Jeff liked to talk with his father, but most of the time his father did not feel like talking. Jeff went to the same school that Sally attended. They had some classes together. They were good friends. Sometimes they talked about school and the subjects they were taking.

Problems

quit *stop*

Soon Jeff and Sally had to **quit** high school. There was just not enough money in either family, so they were needed to help out. They **applied** for jobs at a local grocery store. They were glad when Mr. Blakely, the store owner, hired both of them. They worked hard, but they liked being able to help their families.

applied *asked for, filled out forms*

As the days went by, they began spending more and more time together—talking and helping each other. They became even better friends and soon began dating. After several months as a **couple,** they knew they were in love.

couple *two people who are together*

A Couple

One day Jeff said, "Sally, will you marry me?"

Sally said, "Yes, I will!"

They were married, rented a small apartment, and moved their few **belongings** into it.

They continued to work at the grocery store. Some days it was very hard. Sometimes there were words they didn't understand on store signs and food labels. Numbers were often difficult for them.

Sally and Jeff knew they needed to learn more. They wanted to learn more.

belongings *things people own like clothing or furniture*

Time Passes

As time went by, Sally and Jeff had children of their own—a boy named Sam and a girl named DeeDee.

Sally took time off when they were born, but afterwards she went back to work at the grocery store. While she worked, Sam and DeeDee went to a neighborhood day care center.

Sally and Jeff knew that in a few years their children would start grade school. They wanted to be able to talk with Sam and DeeDee about their schoolwork. They wanted to help their son and daughter learn to read and write well. They wanted to help them with their math and other homework.

Helpful Ideas

Mr. Blakely knew they wanted to learn. He asked them why they did not go to school at night. Free classes were offered at a nearby school.

Jeff and Sally were excited! They found out more about the school. They liked what they heard. They knew it wouldn't be easy holding down a job and taking care of the children, but they decided to attend the classes.

They continued to work all day and went to class at night. Sally and Jeff's families helped out with the children.

They really liked the class and found the teachers to be very helpful. Sally and Jeff found out there were many ways a person could learn. They studied hard.

The students sometimes worked in small groups, and sometimes they studied alone. There were many kinds of books and other things to help them learn. There were computers in the classrooms. The computers were fun to use.

Happy Results

course *group of lessons*

Sally and Jeff finished the **course** of study. It took some time, but they finally earned their GEDs. They were happy and proud of themselves.

Mr. Blakely was also happy. He told them that they were doing a good job at the grocery, and now they could manage the store. This would give them more money, and they wouldn't have to worry about paying their bills.

They liked being store managers and enjoyed their work. And if their families needed them, they could also help their parents, brothers, and sisters.

improved *made better*

But, the best results were that they had learned to read and write better, and they had **improved** their math skills. They would be able to help their children with their schoolwork. They could all have a better life.

Words, Words, Words

A. **Antonyms** are words with the opposite or almost opposite meaning; for example, *up* and *down*. **Synonyms** are words that mean the same or almost the same; for example, *start* and *begin*. Read each pair of words below. On the line, write **A** for antonyms or **S** for synonyms.

1. hot _____ cold

2. noise _____ sound

3. thick _____ thin

4. strong _____ tough

5. cheerful _____ gloomy

6. idea _____ thought

7. wet _____ dry

8. freeze _____ melt

9. help _____ aid

10. enemy _____ friend

Word Story:

The screen is a part of the computer that looks like a TV. It is also called a monitor. Most monitors have color.

B. Some words sound alike but have different meanings; for example, *sea* means *a body of water*

       see means *to look at something*

Read the words below. Then, write a word on the line in each sentence that fits the meaning of the sentence.

by	course	there	two
buy	coarse	too	won
bye	their	to	one

1. DeeDee waved good _____ to her mother.

2. Sam _____ first prize in the math contest.

3. Sally and Jeff took a night _____ of study.

4. Did you go to _____ party last night?

5. Her _____ brother is in the Navy. Her _____ sisters are married.

6. I want to _____ a new blue coat for the winter.

7. Dad will go _____ the grocery store, _____.

8. The child is waiting over _____ for her father.

9. George walked _____ the building last night.

10. The blanket was made of _____ material.

C. The letters **ph** and **gh** can sound like the letter *f*. Say the words *graph, enough,* and *cough.* Listen for the **f sound,** then use these words in the sentences below.

1. Celine had a very bad cold and _____.

2. Mark used a _____ to show the growth in sales.

3. Lucy did not have _____ money to buy a new car.

4. Celine went to the doctor about her _____. The doctor gave her _____ cold pills to last for a week.

D. A *suffix* is a word part added to the end of a word. It can change the meaning of the word. For example: the suffix **-able** means *able to be*. Add the suffix to the words below. Write the new word and its new meaning on the lines. Then use the new word in a sentence. The first one is done for you.

1. tax **taxable**   **able to be taxed**
   The clothes she bought are taxable.

2. pay _____   _____
   _____

3. punish _____   _____
   _____

4. refund _____   _____
   _____

5. avoid _____   _____
   _____

Understanding

A. A *fact* is something you know is true. An *opinion* is what you feel or believe. For example:

Sugar is sweet.   This is a fact.

Sugar is great in tea.   This is an opinion.

Write **F** for a fact or **O** for an opinion for the sentences below.

1. _____ Jeff and Sally became store managers.

2. _____ Grocery stores sell fruits and vegetables.

3. _____ Grocery managers know the best fruits to eat.

4. _____ Jeff and Sally earned more money after they became store managers.

5. _____ Managing a grocery store is an easy job.

B. Use the story and your own ideas to help you answer the questions below.

1. How many brothers did Sally have? _____

2. Why didn't Jeff's father have a job? _____

   _____

3. How many children did Jeff and Sally have? _____

4. How did Jeff and Sally find out about night school? _____

   _____

5. How did Mr. Blakely feel about Sally and Jeff going to night school? _____

   _____

Discussion

A. Read the sentences below. Then number them in the order in which they happened in the story.

a. _____ Jeff and Sally became store managers.

b. _____ Sally and Jeff got married.

c. _____ Jeff and Sally had children.

d. _____ Jeff's family lived near Sally's family.

e. _____ Sally and Jeff went to night school.

B. Read each question below. Use your ideas and the story to answer the questions.

1. Do you think Sally and Jeff will have a better life? Explain your answer. _____

_____

2. In what ways can Sally and Jeff still help their parents and siblings? _____

_____

3. Why did Mr. Blakely make Sally and Jeff managers? _____

_____

4. Do you think Sally and Jeff will make good store managers? Explain your answer. _____

_____

5. Do you think Sally and Jeff will do a good job helping their children with their homework? Explain your answer. _____

_____

LESSON 4

The Best News Ever

FAMILY LIFE

Sheila was worried about her daughter, Jill. Jill was a first grader and was falling behind in her class. Read how Sheila helped her child.

News From School

Sheila picked up the envelope that was in a stack of papers her daughter brought home from school. Sheila didn't look at the other papers but just sat down at the kitchen table and stared at the envelope. It was Jill's report card, and Sheila was afraid to open it.

Jill wasn't worried at all because she had forgotten about the report card. All she cared about was her after-school snack. She was climbing on a kitchen chair to reach her favorite cereal in the cupboard.

"Mom," she said, "I can't reach the box."

Sheila didn't seem to hear her daughter. She pulled out the folded paper and just stared at it. She closed her eyes as if to say a **prayer.** Then, at last, she opened the paper. Her eyes **scanned** the page for a minute. There it was!

Subject	Grade
Reading	Satisfactory

prayer *a humble request*

scanned *looked over quickly*

She read it again to be sure it was true. Jill had a good grade in reading. Sheila didn't say anything, but inside she was **cheering.** At the bottom of the page she saw the teacher's note. It said,

Jill's reading is much improved.

Sheila thought that this was the *best news ever.* She knew then that all the work with Jill had been **worthwhile.**

A Proud Mother

Sheila hurried over to her daughter and gave her a hug. "I could just **squeeze** *the beans out of you,*" she said. "You're so smart, Jilly! I'm so proud of your report card. Mrs. Lopez says your reading is much better. Just look at that!" she said. She showed Jill the note the teacher had written. Jill smiled with pride but quickly remembered her hunger.

"Mom, help me get the cereal, please. I'm **starving**!"

Sheila got the cereal box and watched Jill fix her snack. She seemed like such a big girl, Sheila thought. She was really going to do OK in school. For the first time, Sheila felt sure that things would be better for Jilly. She wouldn't feel the pain of failure.

Remembering the Past

Sheila knew what it was like to fail. She had been a slow reader in school. She was always in the low reading group. School was one long struggle for Sheila because of her reading problems. She always felt dumb. Now as she thought back about her childhood, tears sprang to her eyes. She brushed them away as she remembered that wonderful word.

Satisfactory

Sheila recalled all the hours that she had worked with Jill. It all began after she had met with Jill's teacher, Mrs. Lopez. The teacher said Jill was behind the class in reading. When Sheila heard that, her heart sank. "This is all my fault," she thought. "Jill is behind already in the first grade! Maybe she takes after me."

Mrs. Lopez showed Sheila some of Jill's work.

"She is a bright little girl," she **reassured** Sheila. "But reading is hard for her. And she seems quiet and sad lately."

Sheila knew that Mrs. Lopez was right.

reassured gave hope or encouragement

Jill's Problem

At first, Jill loved school. She would skip out of the house each morning and come home with stories to tell at the end of the day. She was making new friends.

Then suddenly, something changed, and Jill didn't want to get out of bed. She wanted to stay at home. She said she was too tired or that her stomach hurt. It was always something. She just wasn't herself. She stopped talking about the other kids. Sheila asked her about school, but Jill didn't say much.

Sheila thought Jill might be sick, but she didn't have a fever. Sheila was worried. She wondered what was wrong with Jill. Could a little kid *get the blues?* Sheila just couldn't put her finger on the problem. But now she thought she had the answer.

"You're right," she told the teacher. "Jill doesn't like school much these days. I guess she feels bad about her reading problem."

"We don't want her to give up," said Mrs. Lopez. "That's why I wanted to talk with you. We'll give her extra help here, but you can help her, too. Make sure she reads at home. Reading together will make a big difference."

Reading Together

Sheila followed Mrs. Lopez's advice. Everyday when she got home from work and after dinner was finished, she and Jill read together. They took turns reading aloud. They read stories from Jill's schoolbook. They read books that they borrowed from the library. They read poems, **fables,** and stories about people. Sometimes they read an old favorite bedtime story. Whenever and wherever they could, they read together.

They also talked about what they read. Mrs. Lopez said talking was important, too. So Jill and Sheila tested each other with questions. Sometimes they made up new endings for the stories they read. Jill loved to make up **silly** endings. She giggled so much that Sheila laughed, too.

Results

It wasn't always fun, though. Many nights, Sheila was tired and Jill was **grumpy.** Jill wanted to watch TV, but Sheila *stuck to her guns.* Reading comes first, she would tell Jill.

Now looking at Jill's report card, she knew it was all worth it. Sheila felt happy and proud. A load of worry seemed *to melt away.* "I'm a pretty good teacher," she thought. "Who would have guessed it?" Then, Sheila laughed out loud at the thought.

Jill looked at her mother in surprise. "What's so funny, Mom?"

Sheila just smiled and pointed to the report card. "Satisfactory," she said. "This isn't satisfactory. This is **fantastic!**"

fables *stories that give a lesson*

silly *foolish or funny*

grumpy *bad-tempered*

fantastic *wonderful*

Words, Words, Words

A. Sometimes words can be used in a special way. You might say, "It's raining cats and dogs." You know there are no animals falling from the sky. You really mean that it's raining hard. When writers use words this way, they are using **figurative language.** Figurative language helps you to *see* or *feel* what is happening. The writer for the story "The Best News Ever" used figurative language; for example: "Inside she was cheering."

What did the writer mean? Put a √ next to your answer.

a. _____ She was a cheerleader.　　b. _____ She was afraid.

c. _____ She was very happy.

Did you pick answer **c**? The writer was saying she was very happy—so happy that she "felt like cheering."

Read the sentences below. Put a √ next to their meanings.

1. *Her heart sank.*

    a. _____ She felt very sad.　　b. _____ She felt sick.

2. Can a little kid *get the blues?*

    a. _____ get the flu　　b. _____ get a very sad feeling

3. Sheila *stuck to her guns.*

    a. _____ wanted to keep her guns　　b. _____ didn't give up

Word Story:

The cursor is a small bar on a computer screen. It flashes to tell where the next character will appear. The cursor can be moved with the arrow keys or the mouse.

B. The suffix **-ful** means *full of;* for example, *hopeful* means *full of hope.*
Write a new word by adding the suffix **-ful** to the words below.
Then, use the new word in a sentence.

1. care _____

_____

2. power _____

_____

3. pain _____

_____

4. cheer _____

_____

C. The word *ash* has a **short a sound.** Using the lines below, add the
letter or letters **c, cr, d, fl,** or **s** to the word *ash.* Read these new
words and listen to the **short a sound.** Then write a sentence for
the new words. The first one is done for you.

1. c + ash = __**cash**__   **He didn't have any extra cash.** _____

2. cr + ash = _____   _____

3. d + ash = _____   _____

4. fl + ash = _____   _____

5. s + ash = _____   _____

D. Listen for the ending sound in the word *hush.* It is the
-sh sound. Fill in the web below with words that end with the
-sh sound.

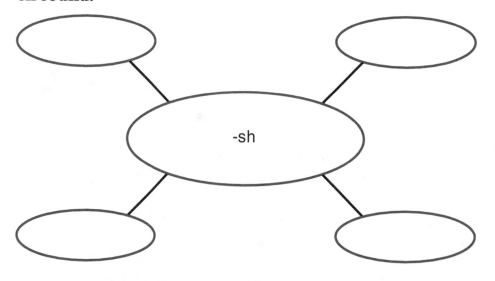

Understanding

A. Read the questions below. Use the story to help you give an answer.

1. How did Jill feel about school before her mother started helping her with her reading?

   _____

2. How did Jill do in school after her mother started helping her with her reading?

   _____

   _____

B. Read the questions below. Use your own ideas to give an answer.

1. Do you think Jill will continue to have reading problems in school? Explain your answer.

   _____

   _____

2. Do you think someone helped Sheila with her reading when she was a child? Explain your answer.

   _____

   _____

3. Do you think it is important to help people improve their reading skills? Explain your answer.

   _____

   _____

Discussion

A. To understand what you read, you need to know *why* things happen and why people feel and act as they do. This means you must look for the causes. For example: Sam was late for work because he missed the bus. What happened to Sam? He was late for work. Why did this happen? He missed the bus.

Read about some things that happened in the story. Tell in your own words why these things happened.

1. Sheila was afraid to open Jill's report card.

   What was Sheila feeling? _____

   Why did she feel this way? _____

2. Sheila cried when she thought about her own childhood.

   What did Sheila do? _____

   What happened to make Sheila feel this way? _____

   _____

B. Read the questions below. Put a √ next to your answer.

1. What was in the envelope that Sheila received from school?

   a. _____ a letter from Mrs. Lopez   b. _____ a birthday card

   c. _____ Jill's report card   d. _____ an invitation

2. Who is Mrs. Lopez?

   a. _____ Sheila's sister   b. _____ a neighbor

   c. _____ Jill's mother   d. _____ Jill's teacher

3. What was Jill's reading grade on the report card?

   a. _____ Needs to Improve   b. _____ Satisfactory

   c. _____ Unsatisfactory   d. _____ Good

A Closer Look at the GED

Sometime in the future, you may plan to take the GED test. Here is some information about this test.

What Is the GED Test?

The letters *GED* stand for *General Educational Development*. This test is also called the High School Equivalency Test. This test gives you a chance to get a high school diploma.

Why Take the Test?

A high school diploma is very important. You usually need one before you can apply for a job or for college. The GED is equal to a high school diploma. With it, you would have a better chance to get the job you want or go on for further education.

How Much Does the Test Cost?

Costs differ from state to state. In some states, the GED is free. Other states charge as much as $35. You will have to check with your test center to find out the fee.

Where to Take the Test

There are more than 3,000 test centers in the United States and Canada.

Who May Take the Test?

You must meet age and residence requirements. A residence requirement means you must live in a place for a period of time.

What's the GED Test Like?

There are five separate tests that make up the GED. Most questions on the tests are multiple choice. Each question has five possible answer choices. But only one answer choice is correct! Some states allow you to take all five sections in one day. Other states allow you to break up the test into two parts. It can take a total of 7½ hours.

What's on the Test?

1. **Writing Skills** tests your ability to use and recognize Standard English. You must also write a short essay.

2. **Social Studies** has questions about U.S. history, political science, economics, geography, and psychology.

3. **Science** has questions about biology, earth science, chemistry, and physics.

4. **Interpreting Literature and the Arts** asks your opinions about passages from literature, plays, poetry, and novels.

5. **Mathematics** tests your ability to solve arithmetic, algebra, and geometry problems.

Trying Again

You can take over again any subtest you didn't pass. The questions will be different. Good luck!

Answer each question below. Use the story to help you.

1. How many test parts are there in the GED? _____

2. The GED can take _____ hours to complete.

3. How much does it cost to take the GED? _____

A Traffic Accident

LIFE AND BASIC SKILLS

Read how Carl learns the hard way about car safety.

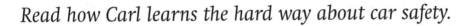

Before the Accident

Carl Dole was driving his older sister, Josie, home from her part-time job after school. Carl was 17. He had been driving for only 6 months.

Carl turned his head to **admire** a new sports car. He wasn't watching the road ahead. All at once Josie yelled, "Carl, watch out!"

Carl looked at the road again, but it was too late. The green car just ahead of him had stopped for a red light. Carl hit his brakes. There was a loud crash as Carl **slammed** into the back of the green car.

After the Crash

"Josie, are you all right?" Carl asked after the crash. He felt scared as he looked at his sister.

"Yeah, I'm OK. Thank goodness for seat belts! Did you get hurt, Carl?"

"No. But look at this **damage**! Dad is going to kill me!"

admire *think well of*

slammed *moved hard with force; smashed into*

damage *harm*

"You should be more worried about that lady in the car. You hit her pretty hard. Listen, Carl, pull over. I'll go see if she's all right, and then I'll call the police."

Who's Hurt

Carl pulled over, and Josie got out. As she ran to the woman in the car, a lady who had seen the accident also ran up.

"Please call the police for us," Josie asked her.

The lady ran into a nearby store as Josie went up to the woman in the car. Her window was open.

"Are you hurt?" Josie asked. "Should I call an **ambulance**?"

"My neck hurts, but I guess I am OK. What happened? Weren't you watching where you were going?"

Things to Do

"The police are being called," Josie replied. "If you can, pull your car over to the curb. My brother and I will wait for the police in our car. We'll get all the information on our car and insurance ready to give you."

"I'll do the same," the lady muttered angrily.

Josie went back to her car. Carl had pulled an insurance paper out of the glove compartment. The paper had a list of things to do. Read the list in the box on page 42.

The Police Arrive

When the police officer came, he took information from Carl, Josie, the **pedestrian** who had witnessed the accident, and Mrs. Lee, the driver of the green car.

He said to Carl and Josie, "I gave Mrs. Lee, the woman you hit, the information you wrote down. Here is the information on her car. Her neck is hurt. She may also have whiplash. I told her to get herself checked by a doctor. You may want to get checked, too. Sometimes you can feel OK after an accident but later find out you were hurt."

ambulance *a car or van that carries sick or injured people*

pedestrian *person on foot in a traffic area*

"Here is my name and badge number. You'll need it when you fill out the accident report form for the state Motor Vehicle Department. And you will need to contact your insurance company right away. I want to see your proof of insurance or **financial responsibility."**

Josie found the insurance card in the glove compartment and handed it to him.

The police office said to Carl, "You were at fault in this accident. I'm ticketing you for not keeping a safe following distance. Lots of drivers get tickets for that." He handed Carl the ticket to sign.

"I'm glad you had your driver's license and proof of insurance with you. I wouldn't want to ticket you for anything else! Your **liability insurance** will pay for Mrs. Lee's injuries and the damage to her car. And your collision insurance will pay for the damage to your car."

Carl Thinks About the Accident

As the police officer drove away, Carl groaned. "Just what I didn't need—an accident! Now with a bad driving record, my insurance rates will probably go up!"

Josie patted her brother's arm, "Even experienced drivers have accidents. One accident doesn't make a bad record. Just learn from this and be extra careful in the future."

financial responsibility *proof that you have the coverage to pay a certain amount if you are at fault in an accident*

liability insurance *the type of insurance that pays for injuries or damage to others when you are at fault in an accident*

What to Do in Case of an Accident

1. Stop at once. Try to move out of the way of traffic. Stay at the scene of the accident.

2. Warn oncoming traffic that there is an accident.

3. Help injured people. Do not move them unless there is danger of fire or another **collision.** Give first aid *only if you know how.* Send for an ambulance if needed.

4. Send for the police. Get the name and badge number of the police officer you talk to.

5. Do not admit blame. Discuss the accident only with the police or your insurance company.

6. Exchange information with the drivers involved.
    - Write down the name, address, and phone number of yourself and the car owner.
    - Give the insurance company name, phone number, and policy number.
    - Give your driver's license number, car license, model, year, license plate number, and **vehicle identification number (VIN)** of the car.

7. Write down the names, addresses, and phone numbers of any witnesses, including passengers.

8. Write down all the facts of the accident. Include the
    - date,
    - time of day,
    - road and weather conditions,
    - damage to **vehicles,** and
    - who was hurt and how badly.

    Make a **sketch** of the accident and describe how it happened.

9. Report the accident to your insurance company immediately.

10. Accidents with injuries or with damage above a certain amount must be reported to your state Motor Vehicle Department. The police will give you the report forms. File your report on time.

If you damage a parked vehicle: Try to find the owner. If you cannot, write a note with your name, address, and phone number for the driver. Put it under a windshield wiper or attach it to the car. Report the accident to the police and to your insurance company.

---

collision *when a car hits something*

vehicle identification number (VIN) *a long number given to each car, truck, or bus to help identify it. The number is usually located on the driver's side of the windshield.*

vehicles *cars, trucks, buses, etc.*

sketch *a drawing*

Words, Words, Words

A. The suffix **-er** added to some words can mean more. Add the **-er** suffix to the words below. If the word already ends with an *e*, just add the *r*.

1. old   Josie is Carl's _____ sister.

2. loud   I do not hear well. Please talk _____.

3. safe   Which man is the _____ driver?

4. new   Her car is _____ than yours.

5. hard   Jake's job is _____ than mine.

6. green   This grass seed makes the lawn grow _____.

7. late   They arrived _____ than we did.

B. Read the sentences below. Write the word on the line that fits the meaning of the sentence.

1. Carl didn't know _____ to pull over.
                       weather   whether

2. _____ until the stoplight turns green.
       Weight   Wait

3. She _____ on a green bicycle.
             rode   road

4. Did he _____ his leg in the accident?
           break   brake

5. The ship sailed out to _____.
                   sea   see

Word Story:

The computer mouse is a small plastic device with an electrical cord that looks like a mouse's tail. It is used to move the cursor on the screen.

C. The following words are **compound words.** Write on the lines the two words that make up each compound word.

1. raincoat   _____   _____

2. nearby   _____   _____

3. whiplash   _____   _____

4. stoplight   _____   _____

5. windshield   _____   _____

6. tryout   _____   _____

7. paycheck   _____   _____

8. turnover   _____   _____

9. backhand   _____   _____

10. outlook   _____   _____

D. Add **consonants** to the letters **-ame** to make new words. Say each new word. Each one will have a long a vowel sound. Then, write each word in the sentence.

1. n + ame   Write down your _____ and address on the paper.

2. g + ame   Did you win the baseball _____?

3. t + ame   No one can _____ that wild lion.

4. sh + ame   Dad yelled, "_____ on you!"

5. fr + ame   Put the children's picture in the _____.

E. Read the sentences below. Circle the word(s) with the **long a sound.** Then, put a √ over the word(s) with the **short a sound.** The first one is done for you.

1. She (gave) first (aid) at the crash scene.

2. He gave me $50 in cash for the watch.

3. Jane asked me to put license plates on her car.

4. I stated the facts and warned them about the damage.

5. Dan thanked Macie for fixing the brakes on the car.

6. The state police officer showed Pat his badge.

7. The lady blamed Carl. Did he admit that the accident was his fault?

Understanding

A. Put a √ next to the sentence that gives the main idea of the story.

1. _____ One accident does not make a bad driving record.

2. _____ Accidents can happen to anyone.

3. _____ You should know what to do in case of an accident.

4. _____ Teenagers are usually poor drivers.

B. Think about what the story says. Write **T** if the sentence is true. Write **F** is the sentence is false. Put a √ if there is not enough information in the story to know for sure.

1. _____ Carl's driving mistake was a common one.

2. _____ Josie did not give any help to her brother.

3. _____ No one suffered any injuries in the accident.

4. _____ All accidents must be reported to the state Motor Vehicle Department.

5. _____ Mrs. Lee was at fault in the car accident.

C. Read the questions below. Think about the story and use your own ideas to give an answer.

1. What might happen if drivers did not have to have proof of insurance or financial responsibility? _____

_____

_____

_____

Discussion

A. Think about what happened in the story "A Traffic Accident." On the lines below write **C** for **Carl,** **P** for **police officer,** **J** for **Josie,** and **L** for **Mrs. Lee** to tell who did or said what in the story. Leave the line blank if no one did or said what is stated. The first one is done for you.

1. ___**C, J, and L**___ talked to the police officer.

2. _____ received a ticket.

3. _____ asked the lady to call the police.

4. _____ admitted blame for the car accident.

5. _____ talked about liability insurance.

6. _____ read information about car accidents.

7. _____ told a driver to be more careful.

8. _____ hurt her neck.

B. Number the following events in the order in which they happened in the story "A Traffic Accident."

a. _____ Mrs. Lee said she was OK.

b. _____ A police officer arrived.

c. _____ A woman called the police to report an accident.

d. _____ The police officer gave a ticket.

e. _____ Josie showed the police officer an insurance card.

f. _____ A car crash happened.

g. _____ The police officer drove away.

LESSON 6

The Yellow Pages

Read how helpful the Yellow Pages can be when you are looking for information.

Special Delivery

It was 5:00 P.M. and Keith was hungry. He had not eaten since 11:00 A.M. He looked around the study room at the neighborhood center. He noticed his friend Susan looked restless, too.

Keith **stared** at her. Susan looked up. Keith waved and smiled. Susan smiled, waved back, and closed her book. Keith went to her study table.

"Are you hungry?" he whispered.

"Yes," whispered Susan. "Are you?"

"Very!" Keith whispered loudly. "I could eat a horse."

Susan laughed. "Horses are hard to catch."

"You're right," said Keith. "Let's go find something else to eat."

Susan picked up her book and went outside with Keith.

"Thanks for inviting me. I really am hungry, but there's a problem," Susan said looking at her watch.

"Is it money?" Keith asked. "I can lend you some."

stared *looked at very hard*

"Thank you," said Susan, "but I'm not short of money. I'm short of time. My sister is picking me up at 6:00 P.M."

"That's not a problem," replied Keith. "We'll eat at a place nearby."

Where to Eat

Keith looked up the street. Susan looked down the street. There were no fast-food places. There were no sandwich places. There were no pizza places. There were no places to eat at all.

"Did you drive to the neighborhood center?" asked Susan.

"No," said Keith. "I took the bus."

"So did I," said Susan.

"Did you see any **vending machines** inside?" asked Keith.

"Yes," said Susan, "but they have just candy. Candy would ruin my **appetite**. I'd rather eat something that's better for me."

"Like pizza," said Keith.

"With lots of cheese," said Susan.

"And green peppers and mushrooms," added Keith. "Do you like green peppers and mushrooms?"

"I *love* green peppers and mushrooms!" Susan exclaimed. "I like pepperoni, too," she added. "How about you, Keith?"

"Susan, a pizza has *got* to have pepperoni! I am getting *very* hungry. Too bad we can't have a pizza now."

Susan's Idea

"We can, Keith!" Susan said as she dug in her purse. Then she dug in her pockets. "Darn!" she exclaimed. "Keith, do you have a quarter?"

"Sure," he said. "Why?" He looked puzzled as he put a quarter in Susan's hand.

"Think about it," said Susan. "Since we can't go to the pizza, we get the pizza to come to us. We'll phone and order one. Do you think they'll deliver it to the neighborhood center?"

vending machines *machines with things to buy such as soda, candy, or coffee*

appetite *the desire to eat*

"Why not?" said Keith. "They can deliver pizza to a home. Why not to a neighborhood center?"

Susan and Keith counted their money and found they had $8.50.

"Do you think that's enough?" asked Susan.

"I'm sure it's enough for a small pizza," Keith said. "I hope it's enough for a medium pizza."

"Me, too," said Susan. "Let's go find a phone."

Keith recalled seeing a phone inside, so they went back in the neighborhood center. The phone was in the **lobby.**

lobby *main hallway*

"Can you **recommend** a pizza place?" Susan asked Keith. "One that delivers?"

"No," said Keith. "The one I like is too far away. We want someplace close. That way we'll be finished with the pizza before your sister picks you up."

recommend *to share your ideas or thoughts or advice with another*

Using the Yellow Pages

"Hmmm," Susan said, "let's look under 'pizza' in the Yellow Pages."

Susan knew the **Yellow Pages Directory** was in **alphabetical order** by subject. Susan opened the directory to the *P* section. She flipped past pages with the word *Pictures* at the top. *Pictures* starts with "pic." *Pizza* starts with "piz." Susan knew *z* comes after *c* in the alphabet. She turned to the first page that had *Pizza* at the top.

Yellow Pages Directory *a large yellow phone book with the names, phone numbers, and addresses of businesses listed in ABC order by subject*

"Good work!" said Keith. "Now what?"

Susan pointed to the first pizza place. "We could call Alonzo's Pizza," she said.

"Fine," said Keith. "I'll read off the number. You dial."

"Not yet," said Susan. "Alonzo's is across town. See, Keith. The address is below the name. Taylor Street is far away."

"You're right," Keith said. "Alonzo's wouldn't drive here."

alphabetical order *putting words, names, places, or things in ABC order*

Keith's eyes scanned the *A*'s, the *B*'s, and the *C*'s. He pointed to the first name in the *D*'s.

"Damato's Pizza is not too far. See? It's at 1122 Prince Street. That's three miles away."

Susan looked where Keith pointed.

"Look. There's also a big display ad for Damato's. Read the last line," she said.

"We deliver anywhere, anytime," Keith read. "All right!"

Placing the Order

Susan placed the call. "How much is a medium pizza? One with green peppers, mushrooms, and pepperoni?" she asked. "Great! Can you deliver it to Harris Neighborhood Center at 30 Wilson Road? Fifteen minutes? That's fine. How will you know who wants the pizza?"

Susan looked at Keith. He pointed to the door.

"No problem," she said into the phone. "You'll know us right away. We'll be the hungry people waiting on the front steps."

Words, Words, Words

A. A **contraction** is a short way to write two words. The (') is used with a contraction. Write each contraction next to the words it stands for.

Word Story:

The keyboard is a set of keys used to type information into the computer. It has all the letters of the alphabet, the numbers 1–9, and a few other symbols.

we'll   it's   let's   that's   you're

1. you are _____

2. let us _____

3. we will _____

4. that is _____

5. it is _____

B. A **prefix** is a group of letters added to the beginning of a word. The prefix will change the meaning of the word. For example: **un-** and **im-** are prefixes when added to a word meaning *not*.

happy   *un*happy means *not happy*
                 Keith was *unhappy*.

possible   *im*possible means *not possible*
                 The hill was *impossible* to climb.

Add **un-** or **im-** to the words below. Use each new word in a sentence.

mature   steady   friendly   practical   certain

1. _____

_____

2. _____

_____

3. _____

_____

4. _____

_____

5. _____

_____

C. The letters **ee** and **ie** sometimes have the sound you hear in the words *tree, see, grief,* and *believe*. The sound you hear is the **long e sound.** Read the sentences below. Use **ee** or **ie** to finish each word.

1. He did not bel_____ve her.

2. Her gr_____n eyes were very bright.

3. They thought a th_____f stole the missing car.

4. Her costume was cr_____py.

5. Keith's answer was very br_____f.

6. The r_____f was very rocky and st_____p.

7. Jo had the d_____d to the house.

D. The letters **qu** can stand for the **kw sound** you hear in the word *queen*. The following words have the **kw sound.** Say these words and then use them to finish each sentence. Be sure the word you write on the line fits the meaning of the sentence.

quart	quarters	questions	quickly
quilt	quit	quivered	quiet

1. She answered all the _____ on the test.

2. The wet dog _____ in the rain.

3. The boy ran _____ down the stairs.

4. Lou _____ his job last week for a better job.

5. LaWanda covered the baby with her grandmother's blue

_____.

6. There are four _____ in a dollar.

7. We need a _____ of milk for dinner.

8. The children were very _____ while the teacher read the story to them.

Understanding

A. Read the questions below. Use your own ideas and the story to help you give an answer.

1. Was Susan wise to eat pizza instead of candy? Tell why.

_____

2. Does Keith trust Susan's ability to solve problems? Tell why.

_____

B. Read the sentences below. Put a √ next to the best ending for them.

1. Keith and Susan will probably

   a. _____ eat the pizza before Susan has to leave.

   b. _____ forget to go outside and wait for the pizza.

2. Susan and Keith will probably

   a. _____ never again use the Yellow Pages.

   b. _____ use the Yellow Pages again to find information.

3. After they eat the pizza, Keith will

   a. _____ take the bus home.

   b. _____ call a cab.

4. In the future, Keith and Susan will

   a. _____ never speak to one another again.

   b. _____ be friendly toward each other.

5. If Keith and Susan ever order another pizza,

   a. _____ it will be topped with mushrooms, green peppers, and pepperoni.

   b. _____ it will be a plain cheese pizza.

Discussion

A. Put these subjects in alphabetical order.

pizza   automobiles   plumbers   beauty shops   dentists

1._____

2._____

3._____

4._____

5._____

B. Use the story to help you. Put a √ next to your answer.

1. What is the main idea of the story part called "Special Delivery"?

   a. _____ Keith hasn't eaten for six hours, and he's hungry.

   b. _____ Susan is studying.

2. What is Keith and Susan's main problem?

   a. _____ They want to use the vending machines but don't have change.

   b. _____ They are hungry, but there are no places to eat nearby.

3. How did Susan decide to solve the problem?

   a. _____ She decided to order a pizza and have it delivered.

   b. _____ She decided to borrow a quarter from Keith.

4. Why does Keith talk to Susan in the study room?

   a. _____ Keith wonders if she is through studying.

   b. _____ Keith asks if she is hungry.

A Closer Look at Getting a Library Card

LIFE AND · BASIC SKILLS ·

Rita Perez wanted to get her own library card. It would allow her to borrow books and videotapes for free. To get a library card, Mrs. Perez first had to fill out an application form. The application form looked a lot like the one you see below. Study the form. Then answer the questions on page 56.

Date _____	I.D. Provided _____

SS# _____

Name _____
(Last)   (First)   (Middle)

Local Address _____

City, State, Zip _____

Home Phone _____ Email _____

Other Address _____

City, State, Zip _____

Other/Bus. Phone _____ Circle: Male/Female   DOB: ___/___/___

Expires __1/2/2000__

Code __333__

Date _____

_____
Signature of Applicant

_____/_____
Signature of Parent or Guardian   (Print name)
(if under 14)

A. Read the statement on the application form below. Then, answer questions 1 and 2 based on this statement.

The destruction or damage of library materials, or the failure to return library materials, or the failure to report lost library materials, or the failure to reimburse for such lost materials or damages is a violation of county ordinance and may result in a misdemeanor punishable by a fine not to exceed $500 or imprisonment not to exceed 60 days.

1. Tell in your own words the different things that can get Mrs. Perez in trouble with the library.

   _____

   _____

2. If Mrs. Perez lost a library book and told the library, what do you think might happen?

   _____

   _____

B. Look at the form on page 55 and answer the questions that follow.

   1. List two types of ID that Mrs. Perez might show. _____

      _____

   2. List some other types of ID. _____

      _____

   3. What do you think "SS#" stands for? _____

      _____

   4. What do you think "DOB" stands for? _____

      _____

   5. Now go back to the form on page 55. Practice filling it out with information about you.

LESSON 7

Smart Shoppers

Li-Li and Fong learn about getting the best buy for their money.

A New Word

The woman in front of Li-Li at the store gave the clerk some **coupons,** and as she wrote her check, she turned to Li-Li and said, "Don't you just love coupons? I saved $23.10!"

Li-Li smiled and said, "Yes," but she didn't know what the woman was talking about. Later that day, Li-Li asked her husband, Fong, if he knew what coupons were. He didn't know, but he told her to ask her teacher.

Li-Li Goes to Class

In class that night, the teacher asked the students what new words they had heard that week, and then he wrote the words on the board. Li-Li gave him the word she had heard earlier that day, coupon. When Mr. Walker looked at the list he said, "You must have read my mind. I was thinking we should talk about shopping tonight. There are six shopping words on this list," he said, as he underlined each word.

Li-Li was pleased that she would learn about her new word in class.

coupons *printed slips of paper that give savings on items such as bread, juice, fruit, soap, or cleansers*

Mr. Walker gave each pair of students a newspaper grocery ad from a different store. Li-Li and her partner, Jamal, had the ad from Save-More.

Mr. Walker asked the class to check their ads for the price of orange juice and eggs, and he wrote the price for each item at each store on the board. The students saw the difference in prices.

comparison shopping *checking the prices on items to find the best price before buying those items*

"This is called **comparison shopping**," said Mr. Walker. "We can see the best buy on the items we want to purchase."

Li-Li read the list on the board. She saw Save-More had the best price for orange juice and a good price for eggs. She was surprised.

What Li-Li Learned

Next, the class talked about Li-Li's word. Mr. Walker told the students that coupons could help them save money and be smart shoppers. Li-Li learned she could find coupons in the newspaper and magazines and, sometimes, in the mail.

She could save as much as a dollar on some items, if the store doubled the coupons. Mr. Walker gave a coupon to each student. He showed the students how to read the details on the coupon. He pointed to the **expiration date,** the size of the package, and where to check to see if you had to buy more than one item at a time.

Li-Li also learned that if she used coupons and comparison shopped, she could be a better shopper for her family. She remembered how much the woman at the supermarket had saved. Jamal told her that Save-More offered **double coupons.**

Comparison Shoppers

Before they went shopping the next time, Li-Li and Fong listed the things they needed from the supermarket. They checked the newspaper ads for the prices of the items at the three stores in their town. They also read the coupons to see which ones they could use. Li-Li and Fong were surprised that Save-More had the lowest prices for most of the items on their list.

When they first moved to town, their friends had told them that Lark's Supermarket had good **value** and low prices. They had always shopped there, although it wasn't near their home. Today they decided to shop at Save-More.

At the Market

Li-Li and Fong took their list and coupons to the store, where they were careful to read the package labels and to buy only the things on their list. Li-Li didn't think the meat looked as nice as what she bought at Lark's. Fong thought their two **daughters** wouldn't like the apples, so he didn't buy any. When they paid for their groceries and used their coupons, the bill was lower than it usually was at Lark's. They felt that they were smart shoppers.

At home, the family unpacked the groceries. The girls asked, "Why didn't you buy any apples?"

"They didn't look good," said Fong.

expiration date *the date that tells when a coupon can no longer be used*

double coupons *when coupons are worth twice their amount. For example, a $.50 coupon is worth $1.00.*

value *what something is worth*

daughters *female children*

The girls were not happy, and during the week, the family found other things they were not happy about. Li-Li saw the meat she bought had more fat than usual. The family liked their regular orange juice better. They did like Save-More's cookies and their **generic** frozen vegetables.

A Class of Smart Shoppers

The next week Li-Li told her **classmates** that she had tried to be a smart shopper. "My family liked Save-More's cookies and their generic vegetables," Li-Li said. "We liked the meat, the fresh fruit, and the orange juice better at our regular store. We liked it that coupons helped us save money."

The other students shared some of their ideas, too, and then the class made a "Smart Shopper List." They all agreed that price was not the only thing to have on their list; it should also have coupons, newspaper ads, and items you like and feel are a good value. They added to check for sales and to buy just the things on their list.

Mr. Walker said, "I am proud. You are smart shoppers!"

At Home

At home, Li-Li and her family discussed what they had learned about shopping. They would make a list, use coupons, and buy store cookies and generic foods whenever possible. They would save and get the best value for their money. Smart shoppers could save at Lark's Supermarket, but they could also buy special items at other stores!

generic *an item with no particular brand name listed on it*

classmates *other people in the same class of study*

Words, Words, Words

A. A **contraction** is a short way to write two words. The (') is used with a contraction. Write the contraction for each pair of words. Then, use each contraction in a sentence.

1. he is _____

2. was not _____

3. I will _____

4. would not _____

5. I am _____

6. she will _____

Word Story:

When you are asked to make a keystroke, you are pressing one of the keys on the computer keyboard.

B. **Singular** means *one*. The *girl* went to the store.
Plural means *more than one*. The *girls* went to the store.

Some words can be made plural by adding **-s** or **-es** to them. Add **-s** or **-es** to the words below. Then use the new word in a sentence.

1. coupon _____

_____

2. student _____

_____

3. dish _____

_____

4. teacher _____

_____

5. daughter _____

_____

6. brush _____

_____

7. egg _____

_____

8. word _____

_____

9. newspaper _____

_____

10. son _____

_____

C. Complete each sentence with the long vowel sound word.

1. Li-Li (made, had) a nice lunch. _____

2. (Bring, Take) your coupons to the store. _____

3. Fong liked the (game, ball). _____

4. Mr. Walker's first name is (John, Jake). _____

5. Lark's Supermarket is a good (place, store). _____

D. The letter **c** has different sounds. In the word *cider,* it has the sound **s.** In the word *cape,* it has the **k sound.** Say each word below. Write **s** or **k** to tell the sound of **c.**

1. cookies _____   2. celery _____

3. class _____   4. called _____

5. cell _____   6. cent _____

7. calendar _____   8. cartoon _____

9. carrot _____   10. cattle _____

Understanding

A. Use the story to help you answer the questions.

1. Write on the lines below what is the same about Save-More and Lark's Supermarket.

   _____

   _____

   _____

2. Write what is different about these markets.

   _____

   _____

   _____

B. Read the sentences below. Put a √ next to the best ending for them.

1. When Li-Li and Fong shop they will

   a. _____ take their daughters.

   b. _____ use a shopping list.

   c. _____ go out of town.

2. Li-Li will keep

   a. _____ Jamal as her friend.

   b. _____ using coupons to save money.

   c. _____ going to class.

Discussion

A. Li-Li and Fong learned how to be smart shoppers. Write a list of the things they did to be smart shoppers. Then, write a list of the things you would do to be a smart shopper.

1. Li-Li and Fong's List

2. Your List

_____   _____

_____   _____

_____   _____

_____   _____

B. Read the questions below. Use the story to help you give answers.

1. What is the name of Li-Li's husband?

_____

2. Who is Mr. Walker?

_____

3. How many children does Li-Li have?

_____

4. At what new supermarket do Li-Li and Fong shop?

_____

5. What did the class put on their "Smart Shopper List"?

_____

_____

You Can
Solve the Problem

You face problems every day. They can be family, work, or school problems. Sometimes you face problems as a consumer. A consumer is someone who buys food, clothes, TVs, or utilities.

As a consumer, you might receive a utility bill for your phone or gas or electricity. Sometimes these bills are wrong. If you have a problem with a utility bill, you might solve it by following these steps.

Step 1   Scan the bill for general information. Study how the information is organized.
- Are there highlighted parts?
- Is some information boxed?

Step 2   Read highlighted and boxed information first.

Step 3   Check the bill carefully. For example,
- make sure the account number, the name, and the address are correct,
- look for the dates of service,
- find the total amount due,
- find the due date for payment.

Step 4   If you find a problem with a bill, call the customer service number right away. This number usually appears on the bottom or the back of the bill.

A. Read the story about Walt Scanlon. Walt lives at 115 Front Street in San Diego, California. He received this month's electric bill. Last month, Walt's electric bill was $35.68. He paid his bill before the due date.

B. A section of Walt's electric bill appears below. Use it and the steps on page 65 to help you answer the questions that follow.

Pacific West Power »»»»»»»»»»»»»»»»»»»»»»»»

Service At: Walt Scanlon 115 Front Street San Diego, California	Questions About Bill or Service, Call **1-631-5550 or** **1-800-555-4434**

Account Number
S1751-5480-00374

PREVIOUS CHARGES:

	Account Balance	Amount Due
Balance at Last Billing	$ 35.68	
Payment - Thank You	$ 35.68	
Previous Balance	$ .00	$ .00
Late Charges	$ .00	$ .00

NEW CHARGES:

Service Period	From	To		
	03/06/2000	04/06/2000	$ 52.20	
	Current Electric Charges		$ 52.20	$ 52.20

Total Amount Due . . . . **$ 52.20**
Due Date   4/10/2000

---

1. What is Walt's account number? _____

2. Is his address correct on the bill? _____

3. The service is from _____ to _____ .

4. What is the total amount due? _____

5. What is the due date for payment? _____

6. Is there a late fee for last month? Yes? _____ No? _____

7. What is the customer service number? _____

8. What are some reasons why Walt would call the customer service number? _____

_____

_____

Sam

Do you sometimes worry about older people in your family? Read how Sam learned how to find a doctor for his father.

NUTRITION · HEALTH AND SAFETY

Sam's Job

Sam worked as a porter in a hospital. His job was to make sure all the rooms were clean. Part of his job was to be the **janitor.** When he was the janitor, he had to clean all the floors and hallways.

janitor *one who cares for a building*

Going to School

Sam was going to school to learn how to operate an X-ray machine. As an X-ray operator, he would have more job **opportunities,** and he would earn more money. With this training, he would be able to use an X-ray machine to take pictures of the bones and important parts of people's bodies. These pictures would help doctors to find out what was wrong with their **patients.**

As a **skilled** hospital worker, he would have to work hard for his salary. However, he would know that he was helping people.

opportunities *good chances*

patients *people under a doctor's care*

skilled *trained*

Learning Skills

Sam was a good learner. He studied hard and improved his English, reading, and writing. As a reader, he read the newspaper every day. He read instructions, his textbooks, and books from the library.

He knew he had to understand what his night school teacher was saying about the X-ray machines. This was the only way to learn and pass the courses he was taking.

Sam and His Father

Sam lived with his father. He cared for his father very much. His father was not a young man. He was getting old. Sam's father didn't like to take care of his **health.** He didn't like to exercise or eat healthy foods. He didn't go to the doctor for a yearly checkup.

health *body's condition*

One day Sam talked to his teacher about his father. He wanted his father to take better care of himself so he would live a long, healthy life. Sam wanted his father to live to see him become an X-ray operator and earn a **degree** in school.

degree *a diploma*

Sam's Father

Before Sam's father came to live with him, he had lived in **Jamaica.** He was a farmer there and raised yams. He believed in nature.

Jamaica *an island in the West Indies*

On market day, he would drive to the farmer's market to sell his yams. People in Jamaica liked to buy the yams because they were as cheap as potatoes but were sweet and good for them.

Sam was born and brought up in Jamaica. When he was a child, he had helped his father on the farm. When he was old enough, he also drove the truck to market and sold the yams.

Sam Talks About a Doctor

Now Sam and his father lived in the U.S.A. Sam wanted his father to get good care and to see a doctor. Sam asked his teacher where he could find a doctor for his father. The teacher told Sam about a doctor who cared for the **elderly.**

elderly *old*

When Sam told his father about the doctor, he was surprised. His father didn't want to go to the doctor.

"I'm too old to be poked and pinched and to take pills," he told his son. "I worked very hard as a farmer in Jamaica. I took good yams to the market. I don't want to run and swim and walk fast. I want to rest and grow old in peace."

Sam **argued** with his father. He told his father that he wanted him to come to his graduation and live to see him become an X-ray operator. He wanted his father to see him stop being a janitor and a porter and become a skilled worker. Sam wanted to see the look on his father's face when his teacher greeted him with respect and pride. Sam wanted his father to be proud of him.

argued *disagreed*

Walking Is Good Exercise

Finally, Sam's father agreed to see the doctor. The doctor was mature enough to understand the elderly man's problem.

"You don't have to be a swimmer," the doctor said. "You don't have to be a runner. You have lived a good life as a farmer, working hard in the sun. You have eaten good foods from your farm. For an older man, you are very strong. And although you are very fit, it is still important to exercise at your age. You must exercise, and one of the ways to excercise is to walk outside. Even if it is cold outside, you can walk around the block. You can also walk up stairs whenever you can."

"I don't like to walk in the cold," said Sam's father to the doctor. "I'm used to sunshine and warm weather. I do not like cold weather. I like to stay inside where it's warm."

The doctor looked into the old man's dark eyes. He said **seriously,** "I hope you will be able to walk to your seat at your son's graduation."

"Yes. That is one walk I want to take," Sam's father said.

"Well, then, if you want to take that walk, you must practice being a walker. As your doctor, I can do my part to help you stay well and healthy. But there are things you will have to do also. Do your understand?"

Sam's father nodded.

"Good. Then today I will listen to your heart and breathing. We will take an X-ray of your lungs and do some simple tests," the doctor said.

"I hope one day my son, Sam, will be in charge of taking the X-rays," the old man said and smiled at the doctor.

"That is what we are all hoping," agreed the doctor. "With your help and by showing him you have not given up on yourself, Sam will do just fine."

"OK. If Sam is going to become an X-ray operator, then his father will become a walker."

Words, Words, Words

A. Read the sentences below. Put a √ next to the words that mean the same as the underlined word in the sentence.

1. Sam wanted his father to get proper <u>care</u>.

   a. _____ attention from a doctor   b. _____ love from a friend

2. Sam wanted his father to live <u>long</u>.

   a. _____ many inches in length   b. _____ many years old

3. Sam's father <u>raised</u> yams.

   a. _____ planted and grew   b. _____ lifted up into the air

4. Sam felt his father should <u>see</u> a doctor.

   a. _____ pay a visit to   b. _____ look at his face

5. Sam wanted to see a proud <u>look</u> on his father's face.

   a. _____ glance from the window   b. _____ expression of pride

B. The prefix **sub-** means *under*. The prefix **in-** sometimes means *not*. For each word below, form a new word by adding the suffix **sub-** or **in-**. Then write what the new word means and use it in a sentence.

   1. way _____

      _____

   2. experienced _____

      _____

3. standard _____

_____

4. complete _____

_____

C. The suffix **-ness** means *the state of being.* For example, the word *awareness* means *the state of being aware.* Add **-ness** to each word below. Then use the new word in a sentence.

1. firm _____

_____

2. still _____

_____

3. dark _____

_____

4. calm _____

_____

5. sweet _____

_____

D. Read the sentences below. Choose the word that has a long vowel sound. Then write the word on the line to complete each sentence.

1. Dinah wears her hair in a (ponytail, braid) _____.

2. They took their umbrellas because of the bad (weather, rain) _____.

3. She wanted to travel by (plane, car) _____.

4. Henry (thanked, repaid) the man for the money. _____

5. The child kept a flashlight in his bedroom at night because he was (afraid, scared) _____.

6. Peter liked to do magic tricks with cards. He always used the (ace, king) of clubs. _____

Understanding

A. The sentences below tell you about a person in the story. Write the word or phrase that best describes that person on the line.

1. Sam studied and improved his reading, writing, and English. Sam was _____.
   a. hard working   b. lazy

2. Sam wanted his father to take good care of himself so he would live to be very old. Sam was a _____ son.
   a. selfish   b. caring

3. Sam told his father that he wanted him to come to his graduation. Sam was _____.
   a. afraid to go alone   b. proud of himself

4. Sam's father didn't like to take care of his health. Sam's father was _____.
   a. ungrateful   b. stubborn

B. Complete the sentences below. Put a √ next to your choice. Use the story and your own ideas to give an answer.

1. Sam was going to school at night so that

   a. _____ he could get a better job.

   b. _____ he could take his father to the doctor.

2. Sam talked to his teacher about his father because

   a. _____ he was worried about his father's health.

   b. _____ he wanted his father to go back to school.

Discussion

A. Read the questions below. Write your answers on the lines.

1. What was Sam's job? _____

2. What job did Sam want to have? _____

3. What vegetable did Sam and his father raise in Jamaica?

   _____

4. Who did Sam talk to first about his father? _____

5. What did Sam do on market day in Jamaica? _____

   _____

6. What exercise did Sam's father finally agree to start doing?

   _____

B. **Summarizing** is a short way to tell something in your own words. Using the story and your own words, write summaries for the statements below.

1. Tell how Sam was trying to get a better job. _____

   _____

2. Tell why Sam was worried about his father. _____

   _____

3. Tell how the doctor finally got Sam's father to agree to start taking care of his health. _____

   _____

   _____

A Closer Look at Vitamins

News stories tell that vitamins help you live longer. There are different vitamins for children, adults, and senior citizens. Find out what you know about vitamins with the quiz below. Write **T** for True or **F** for False.

1. It is best to get your vitamins from pills. _____

2. Some vitamins lessen the dangers of heart disease and cancer. _____

3. Folic acid reduces the risk of some birth defects. _____

4. The meals and snacks you give your children set good or bad eating habits for them. _____

Vitamin Quiz Answers

1. **False** The best way to get your daily vitamins is in the food you eat. It is also cheaper. A banana, strawberry yogurt shake gives you vitamins C and D, calcium, and potassium. And it tastes great!

2. **True** Vitamins C and E and beta-carotene lessen the risks of heart disease. They also reduce the risks of colon and breast cancer. A snack of raw broccoli and dip is a good source of vitamin C and beta-carotene.

3. **True** Folic acid prevents some birth defects. Women need to get enough folic acid before becoming pregnant. Folic acid is found in orange juice and whole grain cereals.

4. **True** Children learn by watching what happens around them. They build good eating habits when you serve well-balanced meals.

What Vitamins Do You Need?

Try to include beta-carotene, vitamins A, C, D, E, and B vitamins when you plan your meals. Calcium, potassium, and iron should also be included in your diet.

What Are the Best Sources?

Look at the Vitamin Chart. It lists vitamins and nutrients with some of their sources.

Vitamin A	Leafy green vegetables, egg yolk, milk, butter
Beta-Carotene	Orange and yellow vegetables, broccoli, cabbage
Vitamin C	Citrus fruits, tomatoes, peppers, berries
Vitamin D	Milk, yeast, egg yolk, and the sun
Vitamin E	Nuts, corn oil, wheat germ, leafy vegetables, eggs
B Vitamins	Whole grains (cereals), lean meat, beans, fish, eggs
Calcium	Dairy products: milk, yogurt, cheeses
Potassium	Bananas, orange juice, apricots, prunes
Iron	Dried beans and peas, bread, eggs, red meat

Create a meal plan that gives the vitamins, nutrients, and iron you need. Use the foods in the chart to create your meal plan. List the vitamins and nutrients each food gives.

Breakfast _____ Vitamins _____

Morning snack _____ Vitamins _____

Lunch _____ Vitamins _____

Afternoon snack _____ Vitamins _____

Dinner _____ Vitamins _____

Teddy's Teeth

Read about the proper care of a baby's teeth.

NUTRITION · HEALTH AND SAFETY

At the Doctor's

"Thanks, Dr. Case. I was real worried about Teddy. I thought he was getting sick."

"No." Sue Case, the clinic's baby doctor, smiled down at the six-month-old. "You're not sick, are you little one? You're just feeling a little **cranky** with those new teeth coming in."

The doctor gently picked up the baby and handed him to his **relieved** mother. "Teddy will feel some **discomfort** as his new teeth start to break through the **gums**."

"Is there anything I can do for him?" asked Dot Swenson as she held the baby who was now smiling at her.

Sharing Ideas

"Yes, you can. You can lightly rub his gums with a clean finger. Or you can use one of those teething rings. Keep it in the freezer to get cold. Babies seem to like the cold and the biting-down action," the doctor advised.

Dot listened and nodded. "I've been doing everything you told me to do since he was born. You know—things about his gums. I always gently wipe his gums with a clean, soft, damp washcloth after feeding him."

cranky *crying, moody, or difficult to deal with*

relieved *not worried*

discomfort *pain*

gums *hold the roots of the teeth*

"That's great, Dot. Many people don't know that teeth care should start within the first few days after birth. And now that Teddy's teeth are coming in, you need to be careful that these new teeth don't get **cavities**."

Dot Tells About Her Teeth

Dot groaned. "Boy, do I know about cavities!"

The doctor looked at the young woman. "How are your teeth? I know you were having trouble. Are you still in pain? Did you call the dental school?"

"Yes, I did. Thank you so much for telling me about the school and its dental clinic, Dr. Case. I did call. They took my name, and I waited a long time. But they finally gave me a time to come in. You were right. They were kind, and the cost was based on what I could **afford**. Look!"

Dot gave the doctor a huge smile showing all her front teeth. Where there was once a chipped tooth, a new tooth showed. Where there was once signs of **decay**, the gums looked better.

"I still have a lot more work to be done," Dot said, "but I don't have pain anymore. It doesn't hurt when I eat or drink hot and cold things."

Dot shifted the baby in her arms. She smiled **shyly** at the doctor. "I don't feel funny about smiling anymore. I only went to a dentist once when I was a little girl. It hurt. I never went back again. I was scared to go this time."

Being Brave

Dr. Case walked with Dot to the door. "I know you were. I am proud of you that you went. It is good for you, and it will be good for Teddy."

The doctor looked down at the sleeping baby. "The way you feel about the dentist and any doctor's visit will affect the way Teddy will feel."

"What do you mean, Dr. Case?" asked Dot.

cavities *decay of teeth*

afford *able to pay*

decay *going bad*

shyly *not forward, embarrassed*

"A child can pick up on how you are feeling. If Teddy thinks you are scared of the dentist or doctor, then he will get scared. You understand, Dot?"

"Yes, I think so."

"Good. Now set up a time with the secretary for your next visit."

"OK. And thanks, Dr. Case."

"You're very welcome." The doctor turned to go to the next exam room when she turned back to Dot and Teddy. "By the way, Dot, the next time you go to the dental clinic, ask them for more information about Teddy's teeth. Thoughts and ideas about dental care can change, so find out."

At the Clinic

During Dot's next visit, she asked the dentist about Teddy's needs. He told her that Teddy would probably have 20 teeth by the time he was 3 years old. Teddy's teeth, like all babies', began to form in his mouth even before his birth.

Dot was surprised to hear this. The dentist also told her that 3 years of age was once the age for a child's first visit to the dentist. However, the new **trend** was for the first visit to take place at around age 1.

trend *the way to do things*

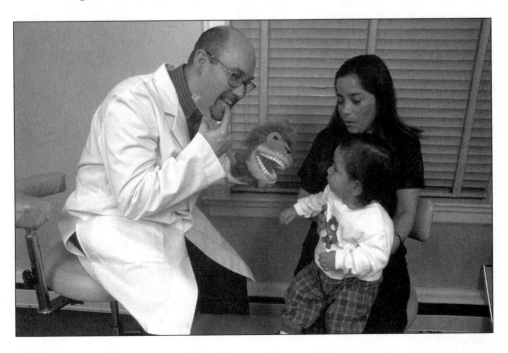

warned *told before something happens*

So Dot set up a time for her next visit and one for Teddy's first visit. Before she left, the dentist also gave her some free booklets to read and **warned** her about something called *baby bottle tooth decay.*

Baby Bottle Tooth Decay

prevented *stopped*

Dot read all the booklets. She found out that baby bottle tooth decay happens if there is always milk, formula, or sugary juices left on the new teeth at bedtime or naptime. This decay can be **prevented**. Some ways to stop it are to give the baby a bottle of plain water at bedtime or naptime and to gently clean the new teeth with a soft **infant** toothbrush.

infant *baby*

Another Visit With Dr. Case

"Hi, Dr. Case," Dot greeted the baby doctor.

"Hi, Dot. Hello, big fella." The doctor took the baby to the baby scale. "Look how well he is doing! How are his new teeth?"

Dot told the doctor what the dentist had said. She told her when Teddy's first visit would be. She showed her the little infant toothbrush she got at the store.

"Isn't it cute? You know something, Dr. Case, I have been thinking about going to school. My husband said he would watch Teddy at night if I decided to go."

"That's great, Dot. What do you think you want to study?"

"I never thought much about it. But lately—especially since my visits to the dentist—well, I think I would like to be a helper to the dentist."

"You mean a dental assistant?"

"Yes, I think so," said Dot.

"That's a good field to get into. I have a friend who is a dental assistant. Before you leave today, I will give you her number. She would love to talk to you about her job."

Words, Words, Words

A. A word to which an ending can be added is a **base word**. Read the words below. Write the base word on the line. The first one is done for you.

1. brushed   **brush**

2. ending   _____

3. thinking   _____

4. greeted   _____

5. starts   _____

6. prevented   _____

7. feeling   _____

8. listens   _____

9. turned   _____

10. thinking   _____

Word Story:

A floppy disk is a plastic disk used in computers to store data or information. Disks can be 3½ inches or 5¼ inches wide.

B. Read the list of base words below. Then read the sentences. Add the ending in the ( ) to a word from the list. Write the new word on the line. Make sure the new word fits the meaning of the sentence. The first one is done for you.

        go   smile   place   brush   eat   read

1. Dr. Case _____**placed**_____ (ed) the baby on the table.

2. The baby _____ (s) at his mom when she picks him up.

3. She _____ (es) her teeth three times a day.

4. Lou is _____ (ing) back to school for a GED.

5. Dot is _____(ing) the booklets about the care of teeth.

6. The child _____(s) oatmeal in the morning.

C. The letters **ee** or **ea** usually stand for the **long e sound,** as in the words *deep* or *each.* Read the sentences below. Write on the line the word or words that have the **long e sound.**

1. Fred will feed the baby. _____

2. Sue brushes her teeth after each meal. _____

3. I want to eat something sweet. _____

4. The geese ate the peanuts. _____

5. Will you clean the spilled cream off the seat? _____

D. The letter **x** can stand for the sound of **ks** as in the word *box.* Say the words in the list below. Then, write sentences for five of the words.

   fix   mix   tax   ax   coax   relax   index   fox

1. _____

2. _____

3. _____

4. _____

5. _____

E. Make the following words plural. Add **-s** or **-es.** Then use the new word in a sentence.

1. gum _____

   _____

2. arm _____

   _____

3. brush _____

   _____

4. month _____

   _____

Understanding

A. Read the questions below. Use the story to help you with your answers.

1. What do you think will be different about Teddy's first visit to the dentist and his mother's first visit to the dentist?

   _____

   _____

2. What do you think will be different about the care Teddy will have for his teeth and the care his mother had as a little girl?

   _____

   _____

3. What do you think will be the same about Teddy's and his mom's feelings about visits to the dentist?

   _____

   _____

B. Read the questions below. Use the story to help you with your answers.

1. Why do you think Dot wants to become a dental assistant?

   _____

   _____

2. Do you think Dr. Case is a caring doctor? Tell why.

   _____

   _____

Discussion

A. Use the story to help you answer the questions below. Put a √ next to your answer.

1. What is the main idea in the part of the story called "At the Doctor's"?

    a. _____ It is important to go to the doctor.

    b. _____ All babies get cranky.

    c. _____ Babies can have discomfort when their teeth are coming in.

2. What is the main idea in the part of the story called "Dot Tells About Her Teeth"?

    a. _____ Dot had bad teeth.

    b. _____ Dot had problems with her teeth that she is now taking care of.

    c. _____ Dot hated going to the dentist.

B. Use the story to answer the questions below. Write your answers on the lines.

1. How many teeth will Teddy have by the time he is three years old? _____

2. At what age should a child have his or her first visit to the dentist? _____

3. Where did Dot go to get help for her teeth? _____

4. What is "Baby Bottle Decay"? _____

You Can
Follow Directions

NUTRITION · HEALTH AND SAFETY

Jamal Williams tried not to panic, but that was easier said than done. It was his first day on the job at the Big Bag Grocery Store, and the man who was supposed to train him called in sick.

Now his new boss, Mr. Gregor, wanted him to stock the dairy shelves with a shipment of milk that had just arrived. There were several types of milk. They all came in different sizes: gallons, half gallons, quarts, and pints.

"This shouldn't take you too long, Jamal," Mr. Gregor said. "Put the milk that's already on the shelves in the front. Put the new milk in the back. Look at the expiration dates. If you see any stale milk, yank it from the shelves altogether. I've got a ton of work to do, so I'll be in my office in the back. You're on your own."

Now answer the questions about Jamal and his new job.

1. List the things Mr. Gregor told Jamal to do. _____

_____

2. List the tasks in the order you think will get the job done fastest.

_____

_____

3. Mr. Gregor told Jamal that it shouldn't take him too long to stock the new milk. How can Jamal find out how long the job should take? _____

_____

4. List two things that could change how long it takes Jamal to stock the milk. _____

_____

5. What can Jamal learn by looking at the dairy shelves before he begins to restock them? _____

_____

6. Why would Mr. Gregor tell Jamal to stock the new milk toward the back, instead of toward the front? _____

_____

7. What is an expiration date? _____

_____

8. Mr. Gregor told Jamal to remove any stale milk from the shelves, but he did not tell Jamal what to do with it. What should Jamal do? _____

_____

9. What should Jamal do if a customer interrupts his work to ask a question? _____

_____

10. If Jamal has a question about stocking the milk, should he interrupt Mr. Gregor in his office? Why or why not?

_____

_____

LESSON 10

WORKPLACE SKILLS

Getting a Government Job

Did you ever think about a government job? Read about working for your city, county, or state.

Local Government Jobs

Are you looking for a job or for a better job? Be sure to check with your local government. Lots of people have good jobs working for their city, county, or state. They serve their community while making a living. For example, the people who **maintain** the roads probably work for the county or the state. People who work for the health department or the police work for local government. The public schools are part of the government, too. You may find **public sector** jobs like these in your area.

maintain *keep up*

public sector *areas of jobs open to everyone*

Types of Jobs

Do you like helping people? Do you like working with your hands? Are you hoping for an office job? Or would you rather work outdoors? No matter what your skills or interests, there may be a job for you. Here are some examples:

- School bus driver
- Office assistant

- School food-service worker

- **Maintenance** worker

- Community service officer—Police Department

- Playground leader—Parks Department

Looking for the Right Job

There are three good ways to learn about jobs in your area.

1. Look in the newspaper want ads. Jobs may be listed together under the city or county. There may be a "hotline" you can call to get more facts about the jobs.

2. Go to your local state employment office. Public job openings will be advertised. Job descriptions should be posted.

3. Ask about job openings at city hall or the county office building.

Facts About Public Jobs

Working in a public job is like working for a large company. Each job has a title and a stated rate of pay. Within one group of jobs, there may be different levels.

For example, there might be an opening for the job of Maintenance Worker II. This job would include certain duties. You would need the right skills and experience to apply for the job. To get a Maintenance Worker I job, you would need less experience and skill. You would also earn a lower wage.

A Maintenance Worker III would earn more and have higher level skills. You might be able to work your way up from one level to the next. To move to the next level, you might need more education or training.

Many jobs have a pay range. For example, an Office Assistant I might make between $7.75 and $9.25 per hour. Each person with that job title is paid within that range. If you don't have much experience, you might start at $7.75 per hour, but you can work your way up with pay raises.

Reading a Job Description

When reading a **job description**, look for the main facts first. Read the job title, salary, and hours. Then read anything that is underlined or in bold print. If you are still interested in the job, read the rest of the description.

job description *tells about the job and its duties*

There is an example of a job description for you to read on page 90. If you like outdoor work, this could be a good job for you. Even if it's not perfect, it might be a good start. You could gain experience and get good **references**. Then you could apply for a better job with the city. If this job doesn't suit you, there are probably other openings. Like lots of people, you might find you like working for the government.

references *people who can tell others about your work and character*

What Is Good About a Government Job?

There are good reasons to think about a public sector job. For one thing, your employer will not go out of business! We will always need our government. Of course, you may lose your job for other reasons, but you could try to get another government job.

Most government jobs have good benefits. If you work full-time, you will probably have health insurance. You will also have paid sick days and vacation time. If you stay on your job, you will probably also have money for your retirement.

Laws and rules protect you. All job openings must be advertised. Job duties and pay must be stated publicly, too. Sometimes it is good to have clear rules about the job and the rate of pay. The boss has to follow the rules. Everyone gets the same treatment.

Finally, like other large employers, the city or the county may help with your education. You might get to study during work time. You might get free on-the-job skills training, or you might get money to help cover college costs.

So if you are job hunting, don't forget the public sector. If you work for your government, it may work for you!

CITY PARKS DEPARTMENT

Maintenance Worker II

Salary $7.40 per hour
40 hours per week

The Maintenance Worker II does many different tasks.
These include

- mowing and trimming of grassy areas,

- clearing of weeds and brush,

- maintaining and removing trees,

- maintaining athletic fields and playground areas,

- painting, and

- installing and repairing fences.

Applicants must be able to work as part of a team.

Applicants must also be

- experienced in maintaining grounds and driving trucks and other vehicles,

- able to use equipment safely,

- able to do hard manual labor.

This work includes walking, lifting, stooping, and carrying.

Applicants must be at least 18 years old and have a valid driver's license.

Apply to Department of Human Resources,
Room 128, City Hall.

Words, Words, Words

A. Read the two sentences that follow.

1. Many people work for the city.

2. <u>They</u> serve their community while making a living.

In sentence 2, the word *they* refers to the people who work for the city. Now read the sentences below. Look for the underlined word. Write the word or words it stands for. The first one is done for you.

1. The Maintenance Worker II does many tasks. <u>These</u> include mowing, clearing brush, and painting.

   The underlined word is _____**These**_____.

   The underlined word stands for _____**tasks**_____.

2. If you like outdoor work, <u>this</u> could be a good job for you.

   The underlined word is _____.

   The underlined word stands for _____.

3. This job offers good benefits. <u>They</u> include sick pay and paid health insurance.

   The underlined word is _____.

   The underlined word stands for _____.

4. Shelley and her sister work in the school cafeteria. Shelley said, "<u>We</u> like to work together."

   The underlined word is _____.

   The underlined word stands for _____.

5. The boss asked Don to work on Saturday. <u>He</u> said, "I need some men to direct traffic after the parade."

The underlined word is _____.

The underlined word stands for _____.

B. The letters **-er** and **-est** are suffixes. The ending **-er** means *more* and **-est** means *most*. For example:

high Jimmy earns a *higher* wage than I do.
Higher means *more high*.

Yoko earns the *highest* salary in the company.
Highest means the *most high*.

Add **-er** and **-est** to the words below. Then use each of the new words in a sentence.

1. long _____   _____

_____

_____

2. loud _____   _____

_____

_____

C. Some words have the letters **ie** or **ee.** These letters sometimes have the long vowel sound you hear in *lie* or *fee.* Read the sentences below and complete the words with **ie** or **ee.**

1. I think you should l_____ down for a nap.

2. Did you s_____ the new building on Main Street?

3. If you don't water the plants, they will d_____.

4. I will pay the yearly school f_____ on Monday.

5. Tom got his dad a new t_____ for Father's Day.

6. Barbara ordered apple p_____ for dessert.

7. Please t _____ the baby's shoes.

8. Joyce was stung by a b_____ in the garden.

9. Rick's brother hurt his kn _____.

Understanding

A. Read the questions below. Use your own ideas to help you give answers.

1. Do you think it is important to have laws and rules about job duties and pay? _____

2. Do you think employers should have to help their employees get more education or training? _____

3. Do you think benefits and job security are as important as high wages? _____

B. Use the information in the story and your own ideas to answer the following questions.

1. Give three reasons why someone might *not* apply for the Maintenance Worker II job at the Parks Department. _____

   _____

   _____

2. Give three reasons why someone might apply for a job that wasn't exactly what he or she wanted. _____

   _____

   _____

   _____

3. What skills and abilities would a school bus driver need to have? _____

   _____

Discussion

A. Read the questions below. Put a √ next to your answer.

1. What is the main idea of the story?

a. _____ A government job is better than working for a business.

b. _____ A government job might be right for you.

2. What is the main idea of "Types of Jobs"?

a. _____ There are jobs for different skills and interests.

b. _____ There are only six types of government jobs.

3. What is "Looking for the Right Job" about?

a. _____ the types of jobs available

b. _____ ways to find out about jobs

B. Read the questions below. Use the story to help you answer the questions.

1. Write two important facts on the Maintenance Worker II job description. _____

_____

2. Write two ways to find out about government jobs in your area.

_____

_____

LESSON 11

The Road to Somewhere

Read about Lewis Payne. He was a young man going nowhere. Then he found a new job and new hope. Read to find out what turned Lewis around.

Time to Think

Lewis sat quietly and watched the others at the Payne family **reunion.** Everyone was eating, drinking, and laughing. It was a good party, but Lewis wasn't having a good time. The boss had cut his hours again, and Lewis couldn't shake his bad mood.

"I can't make it on 20 hours," he thought. "I've got to get another job."

Hard Times

Lewis had been getting by on part-time work since he quit school. He mowed lawns and stocked groceries. He drove a delivery truck for a while. And he worked at his uncle's store sometimes, too. But most of his jobs didn't last.

Lewis felt like he was going nowhere. He still lived with his mother. He couldn't afford to pay rent. For three years he had been talking about getting his own place. He had hoped for a steady job with good pay. But he didn't have much hope these days.

> reunion *meeting or party where people come together after a separation; examples, class reunion, family reunion*

And now he wished he hadn't come to the reunion. He didn't feel like talking. He didn't even try his Aunt Martha's potato salad. And when he heard the others laughing, he just felt worse.

"What's up, Lewis?" asked his brother, Joe. "Want some of that potato salad?"

"No, thanks," said Lewis. "I'll get some later."

"We're going to play some ball when we finish eating. You want to play?"

"I'm too tired. I worked all day," said Lewis as he walked away from Joe. He went over to watch the kids on the playground.

"I wish I was a kid again," he thought. "Kids have it easy. I thought it would be great to be grown up. We used to brag about having our own money and doing what we wanted to do. But I've got nothing to brag about now."

Then Lewis heard his Uncle Curtis telling a story. Lewis used to think Uncle Curtis was cool. But as an adult, he saw his uncle in a different way. Curtis was talking about a new job. It sounded great, but Curtis always had something great coming up. He was going to go to **community college.** He was going to learn carpentry. He was going to be promoted to **foreman.** But his plans never worked out. After all these years, he was still more interested in having a drink than in getting a job.

"Uncle Curtis is all talk," thought Lewis. And then he thought about all the years he had wanted to be just like his uncle. "Well, I am like him," he thought. "I'm going nowhere, too."

New Hope

The next morning he was still thinking about it. On his way to the car, his neighbor, Mr. Walker, called out.

"Hey there, Lewis, I've got a tip for you," he said. "They're hiring over at the Department of Parks. My daughter told me about it. She works in the office. You ought to go over there."

"Yeah, sure," said Lewis. "Thanks."

Lewis wasn't in the mood to talk, but he thought about the job all day. And the next day, he went to City Hall. They were hiring maintenance workers. Lewis tried to read the job description. It had some hard words on it. He told the woman behind the desk he had left his glasses at home, and she read the application for him.

The job sounded pretty good. It was outdoor work, and Lewis had experience mowing lawns and driving trucks. He decided to apply. That night, his mother helped him with the application form. The next day he took it back to City Hall.

community college *a two-year public college*

foreman *person in charge of a group of workers or a part of a factory*

A City Job

Lewis was on the job within a week. The pay wasn't great, but the job was full-time with benefits. Lewis liked his boss, and the boss seemed to like Lewis, too. In fact, when Lewis went to the office to pick up his first paycheck, the boss gave him a suggestion.

She said, "You're a hard worker and a smart young man. You could have a good future if you had an education. Why don't you go back to school? You can even study on work time. Let me know if you want to try it."

Lewis had never liked school, and he sure didn't want to go back now. He knew the boss was right that he wouldn't get a better job unless he improved his reading and writing. He could read well enough to get by, most of the time. But to get a good job, Lewis knew he would have to be able to read directions. He might need to fill out forms and keep records, but he would rather do almost anything than go back to school.

But his boss kept asking. She said, "You could get a tutor. You wouldn't have to go to class."

Lewis thought, "I owe it to her to give it a try." So he made a call to the literacy program.

On His Way Up

A month later, Lewis was meeting his tutor two afternoons a week. They hit it off pretty well. And Lewis felt a lot better about his reading already. "Maybe I'll get my GED," he thought. "Then I could get a better job with the city. I'm on my way. There's no stopping me now."

Words, Words, Words

A. Read the following sentences from the story. Look for the underlined word. Then read the other sentences. Put a √ next to the sentence that uses the word the same way that it was used in the story.

Word Story:

A glitch in computers means the software or hardware does not work right.

1. The boss had <u>cut</u> his hours again.

   a. _____ The plant laid off workers to cut costs.

   b. _____ If it rains today, we won't be able to cut the grass.

2. Lewis couldn't <u>shake</u> his bad mood.

   a. _____ We saw the angry man shake his fist.

   b. _____ I can't seem to shake this cold.

3. "Hey there, Lewis, I've got a <u>tip</u> for you," he said.

   a. _____ Gavin gave the taxi driver a tip.

   b. _____ He got a tip on a horse in the fifth race.

4. For three years he had been talking about getting his own <u>place</u>.

   a. _____ I'm having a party at my place.

   b. _____ That park is not a safe place for kids to play.

5. They hit it off pretty <u>well</u>.

   a. _____ In the country we had well water.

   b. _____ He did well on the math test.

B. Some words sound the same but have different meanings and spellings. Read each sentence from the story and find the underlined word. Then, find a word in the list below that sounds the same as the underlined word. Write the word on the line and use it in a sentence. The first one is done for you.

herd   two   red   new   oh   grate

1. "I'm <u>too</u> tired."

   two   **My birthday is in two days.**

2. I thought it would be <u>great</u> to be grown up.

   _____ _____

3. Then Lewis <u>heard</u> his Uncle Curtis telling a story.

   _____ _____

4. He told the woman he had left his glasses at home, and she <u>read</u> it for him.

   _____ _____

5. He <u>knew</u> the boss was right.

   _____ _____

6. "I <u>owe</u> it to her to give it a try."

   _____ _____

C. The letters **qu** can have the sound you hear in the word _quick_. Say the words below. Use them in the sentences that follow. Make sure they fit the meaning of the sentences.

   quiet   quit   quilt   quarter   quality   quail   quarrel

1. He didn't want to _____ his job and move to another city.

2. I'm going this Sunday to hunt for _____.

3. "Why don't you be _____ and listen to what I have to say?"

4. Lewis met his tutor at a _____ to three in the afternoon.

5. She had a _____ with her boyfriend.

6. Aunt Diane made a yellow _____ for me for my birthday.

7. Sometimes you have to search for a _____ product.

Understanding

A. Read the sentences below. Put a √ next to the best endings.

1. Lewis had his hours cut at work, so he

    a. _____ was in a bad mood.

    b. _____ felt like celebrating.

2. Lewis could see that he was reading better, so he

    a. _____ quit the literacy program.

    b. _____ had high hopes.

3. Because Lewis wanted a better job, he

    a. _____ didn't bother to learn new job skills.

    b. _____ worked hard to impress his boss.

B. Write **F** for a fact or **O** for an opinion.

1. _____ Government job openings must be advertised.

2. _____ Job security is more important than high wages.

3. _____ Young people should not have jobs while they are in high school.

4. _____ To teach in the public schools, you must have a college degree.

5. _____ The employment office has information about job openings.

6. _____ It is better to learn a trade than to go to college.

7. _____ All employers should provide health insurance for workers.

Discussion

A summary tells in a few sentences the main idea about a story. Read the list below. Choose the four most important ideas from the part of the story listed. Write them on the lines in the order in which things happened. Using the chart, write a summary.

New hope
- a tip about a job
- goes to City Hall
- maintenance job opening
- can't read job description

- gets help with the job application
- applies for job

1. _____

2. _____

_____

_____

New hope

3. _____

4. _____

_____

_____

_____

_____

_____

_____

A Closer Look at
a Job Application

In the story "The Road to Somewhere," Lewis Payne had to fill out an application for a job. At the time, he needed help to read it because he didn't read well. Even people who do read well sometimes have trouble filling out a job application.

Applications differ by the job. However, there are certain questions that appear on most applications. General types of job application questions appear below. Read them. Try to get familiar with these questions. Here are also some tips about filling out a job application.

Tips

1. Bring something to write with; a blue or black pen is a good idea.

2. Bring a list of important numbers: your home phone number, your birthdate, and the phone numbers of your references.

3. Bring your social security card and another form of ID.

4. Bring information about your references: full names, addresses, positions they hold, work phone numbers.

5. Bring a copy of your résumé. Since it lists the dates and places of your jobs and school, it will help you with the job application.

General Types of Questions

1. **Date.**   You are always asked the date you are filling out the application. Make sure you write down the correct date. Some jobs have time limits for applying. You don't want to miss out because you put down the wrong date.

2. **Name.**   Print your full name. Do not use a family nickname. Use the name that appears on your social security card.

3. **Address and phone number.**   Print these numbers clearly. Include your zip code for your address and the area code for your phone number. If you do not have a home phone, try to use a number where a message can be left for you.

4. **Position desired** or **Applying for position as.**   These statements ask you to give the title of the job you want. Make sure you give the correct job title.

5. **Date available.**   What date can you start the job?

Here is a sample of an application. Fill it out. Pretend you are applying for an entry-level typist position.

Personal Data   Date _____

Applying for position as _____ Salary required _____ Date available _____

Name _____
            (Last)   (First)   (Middle)

Address _____
          (Street)   (City)   (State)   (Zip)

Telephone no. _____ Social Security no. _____
       (Area code)

Are you legally entitled to work in the United States?   Yes ❑   No ❑

Skills

List any special skills you may have including any obtained in the military:

_____

_____

Business machines you can operate _____

                    ❑ Manual   ❑ Executive

Typing speed _____ words per minute.   ❑ Electric   ❑ Electronic equipment used _____

Steno speed _____ words per minute.   Method _____

Word processing/data processing: Yes ❑   Equipment used _____

_____

A Fable

You are about to read a fable called "The Poor Old Dog." A fable is a brief story that teaches a moral lesson. Fables show how some actions are good or bad, or wise or foolish.

Some fables have human characters. In most fables, the main character is not a person but an animal that behaves like a person. The animal in a fable usually has one main feature and stands for a certain idea. For example, the animal may be selfish. The animal acts in a way that teaches a lesson which is the moral of the story. In most fables, the moral appears at the end in a sentence.

Where Do Fables Come From?

In ancient times, people made up stories about animals that acted like humans. These stories were used to teach moral lessons. Today, we call these stories fables.

You may have heard of *Aesop's Fables*. Aesop was a slave in ancient Greece. He told many witty stories about animals.

For hundreds of years, many writers have retold the ancient fables and written new fables. Fables have spread all over the world. Even writers in the 1900s have written fables.

In the fable "The Poor Old Dog," the main character is just called "the Dog." The poor Dog lives in a park but wishes for a better life. The other character, Mr. Terrier, is another dog. Mr.

Terrier helps the Dog learn an important lesson about life. That lesson or moral is stated at the end of the fable.

Arnold Lobel is the author and illustrator of "The Poor Old Dog" from the Caldecott winning book called *Fables*.

The Poor Old Dog

There was an old Dog who was very poor. The only coat he had to wear was mostly holes held together by ragged threads. He could feel the pebbles on the pavement through the thin soles of his tattered shoes. He slept in the park because he had no home.

The Dog spent most of his time searching in garbage cans. He found bits of string and buttons. These he sold for pennies to passersby.

The Dog always walked with his nose close to the curb, looking for things to sell. That is how he came to find the gold ring that was lying in the gutter.

"My luck has changed," cried the Dog, "for I am sure that this is a magic ring!"

The Dog rubbed the ring and said, "I wish for a new coat. I wish for new shoes. I wish for a house to live in. I wish these wishes could come true right now!"

But nothing happened. The Dog felt the wind through the holes in his coat. He felt the pebbles under his thin shoes. That night he slept on his usual bench in the park.

Several days later, the Dog saw a note on a lamppost. The note said, "Lost: gold ring. Large reward. Mr. Terrier. Ten Wealthy Lane."

The Reading Corner

The old Dog hurried to Wealthy Lane. Mr. Terrier was overjoyed to have his ring returned. He thanked the Dog profusely and gave him a bulging purse that was full of coins.

The Dog bought a warm fur coat. He bought a pair of good shoes with thick soles.

There was a large amount of money left over. The Dog used the rest of it as a down payment on a cozy little house. He moved right in and never had to sleep in the park again.

Wishes, on their way to coming true, will not be rushed.

Words, Words, Words

A. For each pair of words, write **A** for antonyms or **S** for synonyms on the line.

1. poor _____ wealthy
2. trash _____ garbage
3. found _____ lost
4. thrilled _____ overjoyed
5. ragged _____ tattered
6. several _____ few

B. Read the sentences. Put a √ next to the meaning of the underlined word in each sentence.

1. It took only a minute to read the <u>brief</u> story.

   a. _____ scary   b. _____ short   c. _____ exciting

2. We laughed at his <u>witty</u> fables.

   a. _____ funny   b. _____ moral   c. _____ loud

3. I felt the <u>pebbles</u> under my feet as I walked on the road.

   a. _____ cracks   b. _____ sores   c. _____ rocks

C. Some words have more than one meaning. Look for the underlined word. Put a √ next to the best meaning.

1. We saw a <u>ring</u> of smoke.

   a. _____ noise of a bell   b. _____ circle

2. She learned a good <u>lesson</u>.

   a. _____ truth   b. _____ schoolwork

3. Animals have a <u>right</u> to a good home.

   a. _____ correct   b. _____ what one is owed

Understanding

A. Use the fable and your own ideas to answer the questions.

1. What was different about the Dog and Mr. Terrier?

   _____

2. How was the Dog like many people? _____

   _____

3. What is the moral or lesson of this story? _____

   _____

4. What might have happened if the Dog had never seen the note?

   _____

   _____

   _____

   _____

B. Write **F** for a fact. Write **O** for an opinion.

1. _____ Fables teach moral lessons.

2. _____ *Aesop's Fables* are the best fables ever written.

3. _____ Many of our fables come from Greece and India.

4. _____ Authors in this century have written fables.

5. _____ Children like fairy tales more than fables.

6. _____ Arnold Lobel wrote and illustrated the fable "The Poor Old Dog."

Discussion

A. Use the fable to answer the questions.

1. Why did the Dog sleep in the park? _____

_____

2. Where was the gold ring? _____

_____

3. What did the dog wish for? _____

_____

4. What did Mr. Terrier give the Dog? _____

_____

5. How did the Dog find out who owned the ring? _____

_____

_____

B. Read the sentences below. Write **1, 2, 3, 4,** and **5** to show the order in which things happened.

a. _____ The Dog saw a note.

b. _____ The Dog bought a cozy little house.

c. _____ The Dog sold string and buttons.

d. _____ Mr. Terrier gave the Dog a purse.

e. _____ The Dog rubbed the gold ring.

C. Use the fable and your own ideas to answer the questions.

1. What did the Dog think would happen if he rubbed the ring?

_____

_____

_____

_____

2. After he read the note, why might the Dog think Mr. Terrier had lots of money?

_____

_____

_____

_____

_____

3. What is one wish *you* would wish to come true for you?

_____

_____

_____

_____

_____

_____

_____

_____

_____

_____

You Can
Write a Fable

Before you try to write your own fable, read "The Poor Old Dog" again. You might also get a copy of Arnold Lobel's book to read other fables. Then, think about a fable you would like to tell. Follow these steps to help you with your writing.

1. Decide on the moral. This is the lesson you want to teach. You should be able to state your moral in one sentence. Examples: "Don't count your chickens before they are hatched," or "A stitch in time saves nine." Write this moral at the top of the next page. Also, write it at the end of your fable on a line by itself.

2. Think of one or two animal characters for your fable. Tell what kind of animal each character is. Then, next to each animal, write the feature the animal has that makes it behave like a person. For example, a fox can be sly, or it can be a coward. An ant can be hardworking or lazy.

3. Usually fables are named for their characters. Think of a title for your fable and write it on the next page.

4. Think about what your animal or animals will do to teach the lesson. Write down some notes on a piece of paper.

5. Now, try to write your fable. Make it short.

Moral: _____

_____

Characters:

Animal _____ Feature _____

Animal _____ Feature _____

Title: _____

Fable:

_____

_____

_____

_____

_____

_____

_____

_____

_____

_____

_____

_____

_____

_____

Moral: _____

_____

NAME _____ Posttest for Book 5

A. Put a √ next to the synonyms for the first word.

1. rush   a. _____ slow   b. _____ quick   c. _____ fast

2. moist   a. _____ wet   b. _____ dry   c. _____ damp

B. Put a √ next to the antonyms for the first word.

3. enemy   a. _____ friend   b. _____ foe   c. _____ pal

4. freeze   a. _____ wet   b. _____ ice   c. _____ melt

5. strong   a. _____ powerful   b. _____ weak   c. _____ sickly

C. Write the letter **C** on the line if the word is a compound word.
   Put a √ on the line if the word is not a compound word.

6. homework _____   7. public _____   8. nicely _____

9. system _____   10. biggest _____   11. hallway _____

D. Read the sentences. Put a √ next to the word that best
   completes the sentence.

12. Celia is a blues singer. Her songs are

    a. _____ happy   b. _____ off key   c. _____ sad

13. Omar planned a picnic. He was hoping for good

    a. _____ whether   b. _____ weather   c. _____ where

14. Guy _____ the want ads this morning.

    a. _____ red   b. _____ heard   c. _____ read

15. _____ a new child starting school tomorrow.

    a. _____ Their   b. _____ There's   c. _____ They're

E. Read the stories. Put a √ next to your answer.

You should learn to keep your food safe. Food not cooked can cause you to get sick. Raw meat, poultry, seafood, and eggs can cause problems. Before you eat these things, they must be cooked until they are done. Cooked red meat, for example, should be brown inside before you eat it. Safe eggs have cooked egg whites and yolks. They are firm, not runny.

16. What was the story mostly about?

    a. _____ how to cook meat

    b. _____ making egg salad

    c. _____ keeping you and your food safe

17. Cooked eggs should

    a. _____ be runny   b. _____ have no yolks   c. _____ be firm

18. Cooked red meat should

    a. _____ remain red inside

    b. _____ be brown inside

    c. _____ be pink inside

Children need help to learn how to study. Parents can give that help at home. They can aid their children to learn good study skills. One way to begin is to help a child get enough sleep. Many young children need 10 to 12 hours of sleep every night. Serving good, healthy food is another way. These are just two simple ways a parent can begin to help.

19. What was the story mostly about?

    a. _____ helpful parents

    b. _____ eating healthy foods

    c. _____ good study habits begin at home in simple ways

20. What would a good title for this story be?

    a. _____ How to Be a Good Parent

    b. _____ Sleeping Twelve Hours a Night

    c. _____ Study Skills Begin at Home

GLOSSARY

admire	think well of
admitted	told
adoption	the legal process of making a child who was not born to you part of your family
afford	able to pay
alphabetical order	putting words, names, places, or things in ABC order
ambulance	a car or van that carries sick or injured people
appetite	the desire to eat
application	a form written out to give information about a person
applied	asked for, filled out forms
argued	disagreed
bargains	items that are sold for less money
belongings	things people own like clothing or furniture
cavities	decay of teeth
charities	groups that help those who need money, food, clothing, or other types of help
cheering	loud, happy yelling
classmates	other people in the same class of study
collision	when a car hits something
community college	a two-year public college
comparison shopping	checking the prices on items to find the best price before buying those items
couple	two people who are together
coupons	printed slips of paper that give savings on items such as bread, juice, fruit, soap, or cleansers
course	group of lessons
cranky	crying, moody, or difficult to deal with

damage	harm
daughters	female children
decay	going bad
degree	a diploma
discomfort	pain
double coupons	when coupons are worth twice their amount. For example, a $.50 coupon is worth $1.
elderly	old
encyclopedia	a book or a set of books that gives information about many things
enlisted	those who joined the service
expiration date	the date that tells when the coupon can no longer be used
fables	stories that give a lesson
fantastic	wonderful
fast-food chain	restaurants that serve fast food in many different cities and have the same name and menu items
faucet	water tap
financial responsibility	proof that you have the coverage to pay a certain amount if you are at fault in an accident
foreman	person in charge of a group of workers or a part of a factory
franchising	selling the name of a business to other people so they can open a business using the name and selling the products
Frosties	frozen, chocolate dairy drinks
generic	an item with no particular brand name listed on it
grumpy	bad-tempered

gums	hold the roots of the teeth
health	body's condition
improved	made better
infant	baby
injured	hurt
Jamaica	an island in the West Indies
janitor	one who cares for a building
job description	tells about the job and its duties
liability insurance	the type of insurance that pays for injuries or damage to others when you are at fault in an accident
lobby	main hallway
maintain	keep up
maintenance worker	someone who cares for a building
merchandise	items for sale through stores or catalogs
millionaire	somebody who has a million or more dollars
opportunities	good chances
patients	people under a doctor's care
pedestrian	person on foot in a traffic area
prayer	a humble request
prevented	stopped
public sector	areas of jobs open to everyone
quit	stop
reassured	gave hope or encouragement
recommend	to share your ideas or thoughts or advice with another
references	people who can tell others about your work and character
relaxed	felt at ease
relieved	not worried

reunion	meeting or party where people come together after a separation; examples, class reunion, family reunion
scanned	looked over quickly
seriously	not smiling or joking
shyly	not forward, embarrassed
siblings	brothers and sisters
silly	foolish or funny
sketch	a drawing
skilled	trained
slammed	moved hard with force; smashed into
slumped	moved downwards
spokesperson	someone who tells about a place, a thing, an event, a company, or a product
squeeze	to hold tightly
stared	looked at very hard
starving	very hungry
support	help to pay bills
trend	the way to do things
value	what something is worth
vehicle identification number (VIN)	a long number given to each car, truck, or bus to help identify it. The number is usually located on the driver's side of the windshield.
vehicles	cars, trucks, buses, etc.
vending machines	machines with things to buy such as soda, candy, or coffee
volunteer	a person who offers help or works without pay
warned	told before something happens
worthwhile	being worth the time and effort spent
Yellow Pages Directory	a large yellow phone book with the names, phone numbers, and addresses of businesses listed in ABC order by subject

ANSWER KEY

Lesson 1

Words, Words, Words

A. 2. husband 3. smiled 4. proud
5. admitted 6. repair 7. tutors
8. relaxed

B. 3. √ 5. √ 6. √ 7. √ 9. √

C. 1. clay 2. prayed 3. tray

D. 1. shrugged, shrubs 2. shriveling 3. shrubs, shrink

E. 2. performance I missed the last performance of the play.
3. attendance His attendance at school is excellent.

Understanding

A. 1. She was on her own. She had to be in charge. 2. He may have died. He may have left the family. He may be in the service. He may be on a business trip. 3. He was too busy with his friends. He was lazy. He just didn't want to do the report.

B. 1. She might have a better-paying job. She might not have to work so hard. 2. She won't be afraid. She will want to visit again. 3. She could use the newspapers. She could take books out about job hunting.

Discussion

A. 1. She didn't have time. She was afraid.
2. A book about fixing faucets. A book of short stories. 3. They learned about the number system used in libraries.

B. 1. He was angry. 2. He felt bad. 3. He felt good.

C. They were greeted by the volunteer. She helped them. They explored the many rooms. They went to the children's section. Mrs. Perez took some books. She filled out an application for a library card. They checked out books and a video.

Lesson 2

Words, Words, Words

A. 1. don't 2. didn't 3. shouldn't
4. wouldn't 5. couldn't

B. 1. Dave's restaurant 2. cat's food 3. Alec's toy 4. girl's ribbons 5. John's bed
6. Grandfather's car 7. Patrick's book

C. 1. birdhouse 2. birdbath 3. bookmark
4. bookcase 5. checklist 6. checkbook
7. I lost my checkbook. 8. He painted the bookcase. 9. Dora had a checklist of things to do. 10. I used a bookmark.

D. 1. sc 2. wr 3. Sc 4. wr 5. sc 6. wr

Understanding

A. 1. O 2. F 3. F 4. F 5. O 6. O

B. 1. b 2. a 3. b 4. b 5. a

Discussion

A. delivered groceries; worked at Walgreen's; worked as restaurant worker; managed an enlisted men's club; worked at Kentucky Fried Chicken

B. 1. He lost his job. 2. Dave became part owner.

You Can Find the Information

A. 1. 225 tons 2. Frédéric-Auguste Bartholdi
3. New York Harbor

B. The Golden Gate Bridge in San Francisco was designed by Joseph B. Strauss and completed in 1937. The George Washington Bridge over the Hudson River connects New York City to Fort Lee, NJ. It opened in 1931.

Lesson 3

Words, Words, Words

A. 1. A 2. S 3. A 4. S 5. A 6. S 7. A
8. A 9. S 10. A

B. 1. bye 2. won 3. course 4. their 5. one, two 6. buy 7. to, too 8. there 9. by
10. coarse

C. 1. cough 2. graph 3. enough 4. cough, enough

D. 2. payable able to pay The tax is payable in advance.
3. punishable able to be punished His crime is punishable by death.
4. refundable able to be refunded The price of the ticket was refundable.
5. avoidable able to be avoided The accident was avoidable.

Understanding

A. 1. F   2. F   3. O   4. F   5. O
B. 1. 5 brothers   2. He was injured in a car wreck.
   3. 2   4. their boss   5. he approved

Discussion

A. a. 5   b. 2   c. 3   d. 1   e. 4
B. 1. Yes, they will have an opportunity to be promoted and earn more money.   2. They can give them money.   3. They had learned math skills at school.   4. Yes, they are honest and care about their job.   5. Yes, they now have better math and reading skills.

Lesson 4

Words, Words, Words

A. 1. a   2. b   3. b
B. 1. careful   Be careful when you carry the pot.
   2. powerful   The ocean current is powerful.
   3. painful   His broken arm is painful.
   4. cheerful   He is always cheerful.
C. 2. crash   I heard the sound of the car crash.
   3. dash   Put a dash of salt on the vegetables.
   4. flash   The light will flash twice at the end of the song.
   5. sash   She wore a red sash around her waist.
D. dish, wish, cash, wash, bush, ash, dash, mash, rash, rush

Understanding

A. 1. She was unhappy.   2. She did much better.
B. 1. No. Her mother will continue to help her.
   2. No. She had a problem that could have been helped.   3. Yes. It makes it easier to learn and do things if you can read well.

Discussion

A. 1. She was feeling afraid. Jill had not been doing well in school, and Sheila thought Jill's report card would say she wasn't improving.
   2. Sheila felt dumb. She had been a slow reader in school.
B. 1. c   2. d   3. b

A Closer Look at the GED

1. 1. 5   2. 7½ hrs.   3. $35 or less

Lesson 5

Words, Words, Words

A. 1. older   2. louder   3. safer   4. newer
   5. harder   6. greener   7. later

B. 1. whether   2. Wait   3. rode   4. break   5. sea
C. 1. rain coat   2. near by   3. whip lash   4. stop light   5. wind shield   6. try out   7. pay check   8. turn over   9. back hand   10. out look
D. 1. name   2. game   3. tame   4. shame   5. frame
E.
Long a	Short a √
2. gave	cash, watch
3. Jane, plates	asked, car
4. stated	facts, warned, about, damage
5. Macie, brakes	Dan, thanked, car
6. state	Pat, badge
7. lady, blamed	Carl, admit, accident, was, fault

Understanding

A. 2
B. 1. T   2. F   3. F   4. F   5. F
C. People might have to pay for damages they are not responsible for.

Discussion

A. 2. C   3. J   4. C   5. C, J, P, L   6. C   7. L   8. L
B. a. 3   b. 4   c. 2   d. 6   e. 5   f. 1   g. 7

Lesson 6

Words, Words, Words

A. 1. you're   2. let's   3. we'll   4. that's   5. it's
B. 1. immature   He acts so immature, sometimes.
   2. unsteady   The baby walked on unsteady legs.
   3. unfriendly   The dog was unfriendly.
   4. impractical   Her idea about moving was impractical.
   5. uncertain   She was uncertain about the future.
C. 1. ie   2. ee   3. ie   4. ee   5. ie   6. ee; ee   7. ee
D. 1. questions   2. quivered   3. quickly   4. quit
   5. quilt   6. quarters   7. quart   8. quiet

Understanding

A. 1. Yes. It is healthier.   2. Yes. He listened to her.
B. 1. a   2. b   3. a   4. b   5. a

Discussion

A. 1. automobiles   2. beauty shops   3. dentists
   4. pizza   5. plumbers
B. 1. a   2. b   3. a   4. b

A Closer Look at Getting a Library Card

A. 1. Destroying or damaging library materials. Not paying for lost materials.   2. She would have a fine and lose her library card.
B. 1. Social Security card, driver's license   2. School ID, credit card, bank card   3. Social Security number   4. Date of birth   5. Answers will vary.

Lesson 7

Words, Words, Words
A. 1. he's 2. wasn't 3. I'll 4. wouldn't 5. I'm
6. she'll
B. 1. coupons   He clipped out newspaper coupons.
2. students   The students are in the library.
3. dishes   Patrick dried the dishes.
4. teachers   They are both new teachers.
5. daughters   They had three daughters.
6. brushes   I lost the paint brushes.
7. eggs   I made three fried eggs.
8. words   He knows many words.
9. newspapers   She reads two newspapers every day.
10. sons   They have four sons.
C. 1. made 2. Take 3. game 4. Jake 5. place
D. 1. k 2. s 3. k 4. k 5. s 6. s 7. k 8. k 9. k
10. k

Understanding
A. 1. They both sell groceries. 2. Save-More has lower prices; double coupons. Lark's has good value and low prices.
B. 1. b 2. b

Discussion
A. 1. used coupons; read ads; made a list 2. Your list will vary.
B. 1. Fong 2. a teacher 3. 2 daughters 4. Save-More 5. using coupons, newspaper ads, prices

You Can Solve the Problem
1. S1751-5480-00374 2. Yes 3. 03/06/2000–04/06/2000
4. $52.20 5. 4/10/2000 6. No 7. 631-5550 or 1-800-555-4444 8. if he found a problem with his bill; if he had questions about the bill or service

Lesson 8

Words, Words, Words
A. 1. a 2. b 3. a 4. a 5. b
B. 1. subway   a way to travel underground
Tonight I will take the subway home.
2. inexperienced   not experienced
Laura was an inexperienced writer.
3. substandard   not standard
The tools were of substandard quality.
4. incomplete   not complete
The story notes were incomplete.
C. 1. firmness   state of being firm
He tested the firmness of the mattress.

2. stillness   state of being still
The forest had a stillness that was peaceful.
3. darkness   state of being dark
The darkness came quickly.
4. Calmness
There was a quiet calmness about her.
5. Sweetness
There was a sweetness in her smile.
D. 1. braid 2. rain 3. plane 4. repaid 5. afraid
6. ace

Understanding
A. 1. a 2. b 3. b 4. b
B. 1. a 2. a

Discussion
A. 1. a janitor 2. X-ray operator 3. yams 4. his teacher 5. He drove the yams to market to sell.
6. walking
B. 1. He was going to school. 2. He was elderly and might get sick. 3. He made the father understand that he had to do his part to stay well and healthy.

A Closer Look at Vitamins
Meal plan   Answers will vary.

Lesson 9

Words, Words, Words
A. 2. end 3. think 4. greet 5. start 6. prevent
7. feel 8. listen 9. turn 10. think
B. 2. smiles 3. brushes 4. going 5. reading
6. eats
C. 1. feed 2. teeth, each, meal 3. eat, sweet
4. geese, peanuts 5. clean, cream, seat
D. Answers will vary. 1. I will fix the tire.
2. Please mix the batter for the cake. 3. Did you see the red fox? 4. I paid the tax. 5. We like to relax by going out to eat.
E. 1. gums   The baby's gums hurt.
2. arms   She held the baby in her arms.
3. brushes   He brushes his teeth every day.
4. months   We left two months ago.

Understanding
A. 1. He will not be afraid. He will be prepared for the visit. 2. He will have good care. He will go to the dentist for regular checkups. 3. They will both know that the visits are important.
B. 1. She is interested in the field. 2. Yes, she takes time with her patients. She gives good advice.

Discussion

A. 1. c   2. b

B. 1. 20 teeth   2. 6–12 months   3. dental clinic
4. Milk, formula, or sugary juices left on the new
teeth at bedtime or naptime can cause decay.

You Can Follow Directions

1. stock the dairy shelves with milk; put milk
that's already on the shelves in the front; yank
the stale milk   2. yank stale milk; put the milk
already on the shelves in the front   3. time
himself   4. interruptions, if he forgets what he
is supposed to do   5. how much milk is stale
6. so old milk would be sold first   7. last date
milk should be sold   8. take it to the store room
until he can ask Mr. Gregor what to do with it
9. answer customer's question, return to work
10. yes—better to do things right the first time

Lesson 10

Words, Words, Words

A. 2. this/outdoor work   3. They/benefits
4. We/Shelley and her sister   5. He/boss

B. 1. longer   longest
Her hair is longer than mine.
Her sister's hair is the longest.
2. louder   loudest
This horn is louder than yours.
John's horn is the loudest.

C. 1. ie   2. ee   3. ie   4. ee   5. ie   6. ie   7. ie   8. ee
9. ee

Understanding

A. 1. Yes, it allows for fair treatment for everyone.
2. Yes, if they want to have them keep their skills
up to date.
3. Yes, people need to know they have benefits to
help them when they are sick or retired.

B. 1. They don't like the hours.
They don't like the job duties.
They don't have a valid driver's license.
2. needs a job
needs money
needs benefits
3. good driving skills; good driving record

Discussion

A. 1. b   2. a   3. b

B. 1. tasks; where to apply   2. Look in newspaper
want ads. Go to the local state employment
office.

Lesson 11

Words, Words, Words

A. 1. a   2. b   3. b   4. a   5. b

B. 2. grate   He removed the iron grate and went
down the hole.   3. herd   The herd of buffalo
moved West.   4. red   I like the color red.
5. new   Sam has a new car.   6. oh   Oh, I hurt
my hand.

C. 1. quit   2. quail   3. quiet   4. quarter
5. quarrel   6. quilt   7. quality

Understanding

A. 1. a   2. b   3. b

B. 1. F   2. O   3. O   4. F   5. F   6. O   7. O

Discussion

A. 1. a tip about a job   2. maintenance job opening
3. gets help with job application   4. applies for
job   Lewis got a tip about a new job. It was a
maintenance job. He got help with the
application and applied for the job.

A Closer Look at a Job Application

Answers will vary.

The Reading Corner

Words, Words, Words

A. 1. A   2. S   3. A   4. S   5. S   6. A

B. 1. b   2. a   3. c

C. 1. b   2. a   3. b

Understanding

A. 1. Mr. Terrier was wealthy and had a home. The
Dog was poor and had no home.   2. He wanted
to be wealthy. He was impatient for his wishes to
come true.   3. Wishes, on their way to coming
true, will not be rushed.   4. The Dog might have
stayed poor. He might have kept on rubbing the
ring, believing it was magic. He might have tried
to sell or trade the ring for money or other
things.

B. 1. F   2. O   3. F   4. F   5. O   6. F

Discussion

A. 1. He had no home.   2. lying in the gutter   3. a
coat, shoes, and a house   4. a purse full of coins
5. He saw a note on a lamppost.

B. a. 3   b. 5   c. 1   d. 4   e. 2

C. 1. He thought he would immediately get
everything he wished for.   2. Mr. Terrier had lost
a gold ring. He was offering a large reward. He
lived on Wealthy Lane.   3. Answers will vary.